Acoustic & Digital

PIANO BUYER

MODEL & PRICE SUPPLEMENT

Spring 2021

LARRY FINE
Editor

WWW.PIANOBUYER.COM

Piano Buyer Model & Price Supplement is published by:

Brookside Press LLC 619.738.4155
P.O. Box 601041 619.810.0425 (fax)
San Diego, CA 92160 USA info@pianobuyer.com
www.pianobuyer.com

Piano Buyer Model & Price Supplement / Spring 2021
Copyright © 2021 by Brookside Press LLC.
All rights reserved.
"The Piano Book" is a Registered Trademark of Lawrence Fine.
"Piano Buyer" is a Registered Trademark of Brookside Press LLC.

ISBN 978-1-92914574-4

Distributed to the book trade by Independent Publishers Group,
814 North Franklin St., Chicago, IL 60610
(800) 888-4741 or (312) 337-0747
www.ipgbook.com

Reasonable efforts have been made to secure accurate information for this publication. Due in part to the fact that manufacturers and distributors will not always willingly make this information available, however, some indirect sources have been relied on.

Neither the editors nor publisher make any guarantees with respect to the accuracy of the information contained herein, and will not be liable for damages—incidental, consequential, or otherwise—resulting from the use of the information.

CONTENTS

Acoustic Piano
Model & Pricing Guide

This guide contains price information for nearly every brand, model, style, and finish of new piano that has regular distribution in the United States and, for the most part, Canada. Omitted are some marginal, local, or "stencil" brands (brands sold only by a single dealership). Prices are in U.S. dollars and are subject to change. Prices include an allowance for the approximate cost of freight from the U.S. warehouse to the dealer, and for a minimal amount of make-ready by the dealer. The prices cited in this edition were compiled in February 2021 and apply only to piano sales in the U.S. Prices in Canada are often very different due to differences in duty, freight, sales practices, and competition.

Note that the prices of European pianos vary with the value of the dollar against the euro. For this edition, the exchange rate used by most manufacturers was approximately €1 = $1.20. Prices of European pianos include import duties and estimated costs of airfreight (where applicable) to the dealer. However, actual costs will vary depending on the shipping method used, the port of entry, and other variables. Also keep in mind that the dealer may have purchased the piano at an exchange rate different from the current one.

Unless otherwise indicated, cabinet styles are assumed to be traditional in nature, with minimal embellishment and straight legs. Recognizable furniture styles are noted, and the manufacturer's own trademarked style name is used when an appropriate generic name could not be determined. Please see the section on "Furniture Style and Finish" in our online article "**Piano-Buying Basics**" for descriptions or definitions of terms relating to style and finish.

"Size" refers to the height of a vertical or the length of a grand. These are the only dimensions that vary significantly and relate to the quality of the instrument. The height of a vertical piano is measured from the floor to the top of the piano. The length of a grand piano is measured from the very front (keyboard end) to the very back (tail end) with the lid closed.

About Prices

The subject of piano pricing is difficult, complicated, and controversial. One of the major problems is that piano dealers tend to prefer that list prices be as high as possible so they can still make a profit while appearing to give very generous discounts. Honesty about pricing is resisted.

But even knowing what is "honest" is a slippery business because many factors can have a dramatic effect on piano pricing. For one thing, different dealerships can pay very different wholesale prices for the same merchandise, depending on:

- the size of the dealership and how many pianos it agrees to purchase at one time or over a period of time
- whether the dealer pays cash or finances the purchase
- the degree to which the dealer buys manufacturer overstocks at bargain prices
- any special terms the dealership negotiates with the manufacturer or distributor
- the cost of freight to the dealer's location.

In addition to these variations at the wholesale level, retail conditions also vary from dealer to dealer or from one geographic area to another, including:

- the general cost of doing business in the dealer's area
- the level of pre- and post-sale service the dealer provides
- the level of professionalism of the sales staff and the degree to which they are trained and compensated
- the ease of local comparison shopping by the consumer for a particular type of piano or at a particular price level.

Besides the variations between dealerships, the circumstances of each sale at any particular dealership can vary tremendously due to such things as:

- how long a particular piano has been sitting around unsold, racking up finance charges for the dealer
- the dealer's financial condition and need for cash at the moment
- competing sales events going on at other dealerships in the area
- whether or not the customer is trading in a used piano.

As difficult as it might be to come up with accurate price information, confusion and ignorance about pricing for such a high-ticket item is intolerable to the consumer, and can cause decision-making paralysis. I strongly believe that a reasonable amount of price information actually greases the wheels of commerce by giving the customer the peace of mind that allows him or her to make a purchase. In this guide I've tried to give a level of information about price that reasonably respects the interests of both buyer and seller, given the range of prices that can exist for any particular model.

Prices include a bench except where noted. (Even where a price doesn't include a bench, the dealer will almost always provide one and quote a price that includes it.) Most dealers will also include delivery and one or two tunings in the home, but these are optional and a matter of agreement between you and the dealer. Prices do not include sales tax.

In this guide, two prices are given for each model: Manufacturer's Suggested Retail Price (MSRP) and Suggested Maximum Price (SMP).

Manufacturer's Suggested Retail Price (MSRP)
The MSRP is a price provided by the manufacturer or distributor and designed as a starting point from which dealers are expected to discount. I include it here for

reference purposes—only rarely does a customer pay this price. The MSRP is usually figured as a multiple of the wholesale price, but the specific multiple used differs from company to company. **For that reason, it's fruitless to compare prices of different brands by comparing discounts from the MSRP.** To see why, consider the following scenario:

Manufacturer A sells brand A through its dealer A. The wholesale price to the dealer is $1,000, but for the purpose of setting the MSRP, the manufacturer doubles the wholesale price and sets the MSRP at $2,000. Dealer A offers a 25 percent discount off the MSRP, for a "street price" of $1,500.

Manufacturer B sells brand B through its dealer B. The wholesale price to the dealer is also $1,000, but manufacturer B triples the wholesale price and sets the MSRP at $3,000. Dealer B offers a generous 50 percent discount, for a street price of, again, $1,500.

Although the street price is the same for both pianos, a customer shopping at both stores and knowing nothing about the wholesale price or how the MSRPs are computed, is likely to come away with the impression that brand B, with a discount of 50 percent off $3,000, is a more "valuable" piano and a better deal than brand A, with a discount of 25 percent off $2,000. Other factors aside, which dealer do you think will get the sale? It's important to note that there is nothing about brand B that makes it deserving of a higher MSRP than brand A—how to compute the MSRP is essentially a marketing decision on the part of the manufacturer.

Because of the deceptive manner in which MSRPs are so often used, some manufacturers no longer provide them. In those cases, I've left the MSRP column blank.

Suggested Maximum Price (SMP)

The Suggested Maximum Price (SMP) is a price I've created, based on a profit margin that I've uniformly applied to published wholesale prices. (Where the published wholesale price is unavailable, or is believed to be bogus, as is sometimes the case, I've made a reasonable attempt to estimate the SMP from other sources.) Because in the SMP, unlike in the MSRP, the same profit margin is applied to all brands, the SMP can be used as a "benchmark" price for the purpose of comparing brands and offers. The specific profit margin I've chosen for the SMP is one that dealers often try—but rarely manage—to attain. Also included in the SMP, in most cases, are allowances for duty (where applicable), freight charges, and a minimal amount of make-ready by the dealer. Although the SMP is my creation, it's a reasonable estimate of the **maximum** price you should realistically expect to pay. However, **most sales actually take place at a modest discount to the SMP**. How good a deal you can negotiate will vary, depending on the many factors listed earlier.

There is no single "fair" or "right" price that can be applied to every purchase. The only fair price is that which the buyer and seller agree on. It's understandable that you would like to pay as little as possible, but remember that piano shopping is not just about chasing the lowest price. Be sure you are getting the instrument that best suits your needs and preferences, and that the dealer is committed to providing the appropriate level of pre- and post-sale service.

For more information about shopping for a new piano and how to save money, please see pages 60–75 in **The Piano Book**, *Fourth Edition*.

Searchable Database

To search piano models by price range, size, quality level, furniture style, finish, and more, please go to **www.pianobuyer.com** to access the free searchable database of acoustic piano models and prices.

Model	Feet	Inches	Description	MSRP	SMP

BALDWIN

Verticals

Model	Feet	Inches	Description	MSRP	SMP
B342		43	French Provincial Satin Cherry	10,865	7,790
B442		43	Satin Mahogany	10,865	7,790
BP1		47	Polished Ebony	9,595	6,990
BP1/S		47	Polished Ebony with Silver Hardware	9,895	7,190
B243		47	Satin Ebony/Walnut (school piano)	10,865	7,790
BP3		48	French Provincial Polished Rosewood	11,185	7,990
BP3T		48	Polished Ebony	10,865	7,790
BP3T		48	Polished Rosewood	11,185	7,990
BP5		49	Polished Ebony	11,505	8,190
BP5		49	Polished Rosewood	11,825	8,390
BPX5		49	Satin Mahogany	12,145	8,590
B252		52	Satin Ebony	14,165	9,590

Professional Series Grands

Model	Feet	Inches	Description	MSRP	SMP
BP148	4	10	Satin Ebony Lacquer	27,505	18,190
BP148	4	10	Polished Ebony	23,665	15,790
BP148	4	10	Polished Ebony with Silver Hardware	24,945	16,590
BP148	4	10	Polished Mahogany/Walnut/White	24,945	16,590
BP152	5		Satin Ebony Lacquer	30,705	20,190
BP152	5		Polished Ebony	26,865	17,790
BP152	5		Polished Mahogany/Walnut/White	28,145	18,590
BP165	5	5	Satin Ebony Lacquer	32,945	21,590
BP165	5	5	Polished Ebony	29,425	19,390
BP165	5	5	Polished Ebony with Silver Hardware	30,705	20,190
BP165	5	5	Polished Mahogany/Walnut/White	30,705	20,190
BP178	5	10	Satin Ebony Lacquer	43,825	28,390
BP178	5	10	Polished Ebony	39,665	25,790
BP178	5	10	Polished Mahogany/Walnut	41,265	26,790
BP190	6	3	Satin Ebony Lacquer	51,825	33,390
BP190	6	3	Polished Ebony	47,345	30,590
BP190	6	3	Polished Mahogany/Walnut	49,265	31,790
BP211	6	11	Polished Ebony	70,385	44,990

Academy Series Grands

Model	Feet	Inches	Description	MSRP	SMP
BA146	4	9	Satin Ebony	22,385	14,990
BA146	4	9	Polished Ebony	20,785	13,990
BA146	4	9	Polished Ebony with Silver Hardware	22,385	14,990
BA146	4	9	Polished Mahogany/Walnut/White	22,385	14,990
BA151	5		Satin Ebony	24,945	16,590
BA151	5		Polished Ebony	23,345	15,590
BA151	5		Polished Ebony with Silver Hardware	24,945	16,590
BA151	5		Polished Mahogany/Walnut/White	24,945	16,590
BA161	5	4	Satin Ebony	27,185	17,990
BA161	5	4	Polished Ebony	25,585	16,990
BA161	5	4	Polished Ebony with Silver Hardware	27,185	17,990
BA161	5	4	Polished Mahogany/Walnut/White	27,185	17,990

Model	Feet	Inches	Description	MSRP	SMP

BALDWIN *(continued)*

Model	Feet	Inches	Description	MSRP	SMP
BA177	5	9	Satin Ebony	33,585	21,990
BA177	5	9	Polished Ebony	31,985	20,990
BA177	5	9	Polished Mahogany/Walnut	33,585	21,990
BA186	6	1	Satin Ebony	39,985	25,990
BA186	6	1	Polished Ebony	38,385	24,990
BA217	7	1	Polished Ebony	51,185	32,990

BECHSTEIN, C.

C. Bechstein Academy Series Verticals

Model	Feet	Inches	Description	MSRP	SMP
A114 Modern		44	Polished Ebony	25,900	25,750
A114 Modern		44	Polished White	28,900	28,652
A114 Chrome Art		44	Polished Ebony	27,900	27,201
A114 Chrome Art		44	Polished White	29,900	29,628
A114 Compact		45.5	Polished Ebony	26,900	25,750
A114 Compact		45.5	Polished White	28,900	28,652
A116 Compact		45.5	Satin and Polished Walnut/Mahogany/Cherry	30,900	30,103
A124 Imposant		49	Polished Ebony	28,900	28,217
A124 Imposant		49	Polished White	31,900	31,119
A124 Style		49.5	Polished Ebony	29,900	29,668
A124 Style		49.5	Polished White	33,900	32,569
A124 Style		49.5	Satin and Polished Mahogany/Walnut/Cherry	34,900	34,020

C. Bechstein Verticals

Model	Feet	Inches	Description	MSRP	SMP
Millenium 116K		46	Polished Ebony	30,900	30,305
Millenium 116K		46	Polished White	33,900	33,418
Classic 118		46.5	Polished Ebony	32,900	31,861
Classic 118		46.5	Polished White	34,900	34,712
Classic 118		46.5	Satin and Polished Walnut/Mahogany/Cherry	36,900	36,531
Contour 118		46.5	Polished Ebony	33,900	33,418
Contour 118		46.5	Polished White	36,900	36,531
Contour 118		46.5	Satin and Polished Walnut/Mahogany/Cherry	37,900	37,798
Classic 124		49	Polished Ebony	38,900	38,087
Classic 124		49	Polished White	42,900	41,200
Classic 124		49	Satin and Polished Walnut/Mahogany/Cherry	43,900	42,757
Elegance 124		49	Polished Ebony	39,900	39,644
Elegance 124		49	Polished White	43,900	42,757
Elegance 124		49	Satin and Polished Walnut/Mahogany/Cherry	44,900	44,313
Concert 8		51.5	Polished Ebony	70,900	67,457
Concert 8		51.5	Polished White	73,900	68,969
Concert 8		51.5	Polished Walnut/Mahogany	76,900	70,481
Concert 8		51.5	Polished Burl Walnut	79,900	73,505
Concert 8		51.5	Polished Cherry w/Inlays	82,900	82,089

C. Bechstein Academy Series Grands

Model	Feet	Inches	Description	MSRP	SMP
A160	5	3	Polished Ebony	65,900	62,434
A160	5	3	Satin and Polished Mahogany/Walnut	75,900	73,330

PIANOBUYER *Model & Price Supplement*

Model	Feet	Inches	Description	MSRP	SMP

BECHSTEIN, C. *(continued)*

Model	Feet	Inches	Description	MSRP	SMP
A160	5	3	Polished White	72,900	69,104
A175	5	9	Polished Ebony	69,900	67,104
A175	5	9	Satin and Polished Walnut/Mahogany	79,900	77,999
A175	5	9	Polished White	76,900	73,773
A190	6	3	Polished Ebony	73,900	71,773
A190	6	3	Satin and Polished Mahogany/Walnut	83,900	82,669
A190	6	3	Polished White	79,900	76,443
A208	6	8	Polished Ebony	81,900	77,999
A208	6	8	Satin and Polished Mahogany/Walnut	91,900	91,564
A208	6	8	Polished White	88,900	84,669
A228	7	5	Polished Ebony	93,900	89,338
A228	7	5	Satin and Polished Mahogany/Walnut	103,900	103,617
A228	7	5	Polished White	99,900	95,564

C. Bechstein Grands

Model	Feet	Inches	Description	MSRP	SMP
L167	5	6	Polished Ebony	125,900	110,841
L167	5	6	Satin and Polished Mahogany/Walnut/Cherry	143,900	125,961
L167	5	6	Polished White	131,900	115,377
A192	6	4	Polished Ebony	148,900	130,498
A192	6	4	Satin and Polished Mahogany/Walnut/Cherry	166,900	145,618
A192	6	4	Polished White	156,900	138,058
B212	6	11	Polished Ebony	170,900	150,154
B212	6	11	Polished White	178,900	157,714
C234	7	7	Polished Ebony	199,900	167,094
C234	7	7	Polished White	219,900	175,551
D282	9	2	Polished Ebony	269,900	216,426
D282	9	2	Polished White	285,900	227,702

BLÜTHNER

Prices do not include bench.

Verticals

Model	Feet	Inches	Description	MSRP	SMP
D		45	Satin and Polished Ebony	34,648	32,356
D		45	Satin and Polished Walnut/Mahogany	37,420	34,864
D		45	Satin and Polished Cherry	37,594	35,022
D		45	Satin and Polished White	37,074	34,551
D		45	Satin and Polished Bubinga/Yew/Rosewood/Macassar	38,460	35,805
C		46	Satin and Polished Ebony	38,498	35,840
C		46	Satin and Polished Mahogany/Walnut	41,578	38,627
C		46	Satin and Polished Cherry	41,771	38,802
C		46	Satin and Polished White	41,193	38,279
C		46	Satin and Polished Bubinga/Yew/Rosewood/Macassar	42,733	39,672
C		46	Saxony Polished Pyramid Mahogany	48,893	45,247
C		46	Polished Burl Walnut/Camphor	51,973	48,034
A		49	Satin and Polished Ebony	44,357	41,142
A		49	Satin and Polished Mahogany/Walnut	47,905	44,353

Model	Feet	Inches	Description	MSRP	SMP
BLÜTHNER *(continued)*					
A		49	Satin and Polished Cherry	48,127	44,554
A		49	Satin and Polished White	47,462	43,952
A		49	Satin and Polished Bubinga/Yew/Rosewood/Macassar	49,236	45,557
A		49	Saxony Polished Pyramid Mahogany	56,333	51,980
A		49	Polished Burl Walnut/Camphor	59,882	55,192
B		52	Satin and Polished Ebony	50,215	46,443
B		52	Satin and Polished Mahogany/Walnut	54,232	50,079
B		52	Satin and Polished Cherry	54,483	50,306
B		52	Satin and Polished White	53,730	49,624
B		52	Satin and Polished Bubinga/Yew/Rosewood/Macassar	55,739	51,443
B		52	Saxony Polished Pyramid Mahogany	63,773	58,713
B		52	Polished Burl Walnut/Camphor	67,790	62,348
S		57.5	Satin and Polished Ebony	67,479	62,067
S		57.5	Satin and Polished Mahogany/Walnut	72,878	66,953
S		57.5	Satin and Polished Cherry	73,215	67,258
S		57.5	Satin and Polished White	72,203	66,342
S		57.5	Satin and Polished Bubinga/Yew/Rosewood/Macassar	74,902	68,785
S		57.5	Saxony Polished Pyramid Mahogany	85,699	78,556
S		57.5	Polished Burl Walnut/Camphor	91,097	83,441
Verticals			e-volution Hybrid Piano System, add	8,200	7,421
Verticals			Sostenuto, add	3,400	3,077
Grands					
11	5	1	Satin and Polished Ebony	86,874	79,619
11	5	1	Satin and Polished Mahogany/Walnut	93,824	85,909
11	5	1	Satin and Polished Cherry	94,258	86,301
11	5	1	Satin and Polished White	92,955	85,122
11	5	1	Satin and Polished Bubinga/Yew/Rosewood/Macassar	96,430	88,267
11	5	1	Saxony Polished Pyramid Mahogany	111,199	101,633
11	5	1	Polished Burl Walnut/Camphor	111,199	101,633
11	5	1	President Polished Ebony	98,462	90,106
11	5	1	President Polished Mahogany/Walnut	105,412	96,395
11	5	1	President Polished Bubinga	108,018	98,754
11	5	1	President Burl Walnut	122,787	112,119
11	5	1	Wilhelm II Satin and Polished Ebony	101,642	92,984
11	5	1	Wilhelm II Polished Mahogany/Walnut	109,774	100,343
11	5	1	Wilhelm II Polished Pyramid Mahogany	129,225	117,946
11	5	1	Wilhelm II Polished Burl Walnut	129,225	117,946
11	5	1	Ambassador Santos Rosewood	125,359	114,447
11	5	1	Ambassador Walnut	121,971	111,381
11	5	1	Nicolas II Satin Walnut with Burl Inlay	124,542	113,708
11	5	1	Louis XIV Rococo Satin White with Gold	139,433	127,184
11	5	1	Jubilee Polished Ebony	104,900	95,932
11	5	1	Jubilee Polished Mahogany/Walnut	111,850	102,222
11	5	1	Julius Bluthner Edition	107,837	98,590
11	5	1	Crystal Edition Elegance	131,979	120,438

Model	Feet	Inches	Description	MSRP	SMP
BLÜTHNER *(continued)*					
11	5	1	Crystal Edition Idyllic	154,512	140,830
PH	5	1	Paul Hennigsen Design	129,000	117,742
10	5	5	Satin and Polished Ebony	100,146	91,630
10	5	5	Satin and Polished Mahogany/Walnut	108,158	98,881
10	5	5	Satin and Polished Cherry	108,659	99,334
10	5	5	Satin and Polished White	107,156	97,974
10	5	5	Satin and Polished Bubinga/Yew/Rosewood/Macassar	111,162	101,599
10	5	5	Saxony Polished Pyramid Mahogany	126,184	115,194
10	5	5	Polished Burl Walnut/Camphor	126,184	115,194
10	5	5	President Polished Ebony	111,735	102,118
10	5	5	President Polished Mahogany/Walnut	119,746	109,367
10	5	5	President Polished Bubinga	122,751	112,087
10	5	5	President Burl Walnut	137,773	125,681
10	5	5	Senator Walnut w/Leather	115,884	105,872
10	5	5	Senator Jacaranda Satin Rosewood w/Leather	125,541	114,612
10	5	5	Wilhelm II Satin and Polished Ebony	117,171	107,037
10	5	5	Wilhelm II Polished Mahogany/Walnut	126,545	115,520
10	5	5	Wilhelm II Polished Pyramid Mahogany	144,211	131,508
10	5	5	Wilhelm II Polished Burl Walnut	144,211	131,508
10	5	5	Ambassador Santos Rosewood	144,511	131,779
10	5	5	Ambassador Walnut	140,605	128,244
10	5	5	Nicolas II Satin Walnut with Burl Inlay	138,803	126,614
10	5	5	Louis XIV Rococo Satin White with Gold	160,735	146,462
10	5	5	Jubilee Polished Ebony	118,173	107,944
10	5	5	Jubilee Polished Mahogany/Walnut	126,184	115,194
10	5	5	Dynasty	144,211	131,508
10	5	5	Julius Bluthner Edition	119,103	108,786
10	5	5	Crystal Edition Elegance	144,855	132,090
10	5	5	Crystal Edition Idyllic	167,388	152,482
PH	5	9	Paul Hennigsen Design	169,000	153,941
6	6	3	Satin and Polished Ebony	113,868	104,048
6	6	3	Satin and Polished Mahogany/Walnut	122,977	112,291
6	6	3	Satin and Polished Cherry	123,546	112,806
6	6	3	Satin and Polished White	121,838	111,261
6	6	3	Satin and Polished Bubinga/Yew/Rosewood/Macassar	126,393	115,383
6	6	3	Saxony Polished Pyramid Mahogany	143,473	130,840
6	6	3	Polished Burl Walnut/Camphor	143,473	130,840
6	6	3	President Polished Ebony	125,456	114,535
6	6	3	President Polished Mahogany/Walnut	134,565	122,778
6	6	3	President Polished Bubinga	137,981	125,870
6	6	3	President Burl Walnut	155,062	141,328
6	6	3	Senator Walnut w/Leather	128,760	117,525
6	6	3	Senator Jacaranda Satin Rosewood w/Leather	138,417	126,264
6	6	3	Wilhelm II Satin and Polished Ebony	133,225	121,566
6	6	3	Wilhelm II Polished Mahogany/Walnut	143,883	131,211

Model	Feet	Inches	Description	MSRP	SMP
BLÜTHNER *(continued)*					
6	6	3	Wilhelm II Polished Pyramid Mahogany	161,500	147,154
6	6	3	Wilhelm II Polished Burl Walnut	161,500	147,154
6	6	3	Ambassador Santos Rosewood	156,727	142,834
6	6	3	Ambassador Walnut	153,721	140,114
6	6	3	Nicolas II Satin Walnut with Burl Inlay	157,821	143,824
6	6	3	Louis XIV Rococo Satin White with Gold	182,758	166,392
6	6	3	Jubilee Polished Ebony	131,894	120,361
6	6	3	Jubilee Polished Mahogany/Walnut	141,003	128,605
6	6	3	Dynasty	161,500	147,154
6	6	3	Julius Bluthner Edition	125,874	114,913
6	6	3	Crystal Edition Elegance	159,840	145,652
6	6	3	Crystal Edition Idyllic	199,800	181,814
6	6	3	Jubilee Plate, add	5,794	5,243
4	6	10	Satin and Polished Ebony	133,962	122,233
4	6	10	Satin and Polished Mahogany/Walnut	144,679	131,931
4	6	10	Satin and Polished Cherry	145,349	132,538
4	6	10	Satin and Polished White	143,339	130,719
4	6	10	Satin and Polished Bubinga/Yew/Rosewood/Macassar	148,698	135,568
4	6	10	Saxony Polished Pyramid Mahogany	168,792	153,753
4	6	10	Polished Burl Walnut/Camphor	168,792	153,753
4	6	10	President Polished Ebony	145,550	132,719
4	6	10	President Polished Mahogany/Walnut	156,267	142,418
4	6	10	President Polished Bubinga	160,286	146,055
4	6	10	President Burl Walnut	180,380	164,240
4	6	10	Senator Walnut w/Leather	148,074	135,004
4	6	10	Senator Jacaranda Satin Rosewood w/Leather	157,731	143,743
4	6	10	Wilhelm II Satin and Polished Ebony	156,735	142,842
4	6	10	Wilhelm II Polished Mahogany/Walnut	169,274	154,189
4	6	10	Wilhelm II Polished Pyramid Mahogany	186,818	170,066
4	6	10	Wilhelm II Polished Burl Walnut	186,818	170,066
4	6	10	Ambassador Santos Rosewood	181,411	165,173
4	6	10	Ambassador Walnut	176,508	160,736
4	6	10	Nicolas II Satin Walnut with Burl Inlay	185,671	169,028
4	6	10	Louis XIV Rococo Satin White with Gold	215,009	195,578
4	6	10	Jubilee Polished Ebony	151,988	138,546
4	6	10	Jubilee Polished Mahogany/Walnut	162,705	148,244
4	6	10	Dynasty	186,818	170,066
4	6	10	Julius Bluthner Edition	152,903	139,374
4	6	10	Queen Victoria JB Edition Polished Rosewood	183,000	166,611
4	6	10	Crystal Edition Elegance	177,045	161,222
4	6	10	Crystal Edition Idyllic	218,892	199,092
2	7	8	Satin and Polished Ebony	150,707	137,386
2	7	8	Satin and Polished Mahogany/Walnut	162,764	148,298
2	7	8	Satin and Polished Cherry	163,517	148,979
2	7	8	Satin and Polished White	161,257	146,934

Model	Feet	Inches	Description	MSRP	SMP
BLÜTHNER *(continued)*					
2	7	8	Satin and Polished Bubinga/Yew/Rosewood/Macassar	167,285	152,389
2	7	8	Saxony Polished Pyramid Mahogany	191,398	174,211
2	7	8	Polished Burl Walnut/Camphor	191,398	174,211
2	7	8	President Polished Ebony	162,296	147,874
2	7	8	President Polished Mahogany/Walnut	174,352	158,785
2	7	8	President Polished Bubinga	178,873	162,876
2	7	8	President Burl Walnut	202,986	184,698
2	7	8	Senator Walnut w/Leather	160,950	146,656
2	7	8	Senator Jacaranda Satin Rosewood w/Leather	170,607	155,395
2	7	8	Wilhelm II Satin and Polished Ebony	176,327	160,572
2	7	8	Wilhelm II Polished Mahogany/Walnut	190,434	173,338
2	7	8	Wilhelm II Polished Pyramid Mahogany	209,424	190,524
2	7	8	Wilhelm II Polished Burl Walnut	209,424	190,524
2	7	8	Ambassador Santos Rosewood	204,088	185,695
2	7	8	Ambassador Walnut	198,572	180,703
2	7	8	Nicolas II Satin Walnut with Burl Inlay	210,538	191,532
2	7	8	Louis XIV Rococo Satin White with Gold	241,885	219,900
2	7	8	Jubilee Polished Ebony	168,734	153,700
2	7	8	Jubilee Polished Mahogany/Walnut	180,790	164,611
2	7	8	Dynasty	209,424	190,524
2	7	8	Julius Bluthner Edition	177,045	161,222
2	7	8	Queen Victoria JB Edition Polished Rosewood	202,456	184,218
2	7	8	Crystal Edition Elegance	231,768	210,745
2	7	8	Crystal Edition Idyllic	273,615	248,615
1	9	2	Satin and Polished Ebony	203,253	184,939
1	9	2	Satin and Polished Mahogany/Walnut	219,513	199,654
1	9	2	Satin and Polished Cherry	220,529	200,574
1	9	2	Satin and Polished White	217,480	197,814
1	9	2	Satin and Polished Bubinga/Yew/Rosewood/Macassar	225,610	205,172
1	9	2	Saxony Polished Pyramid Mahogany	258,131	234,603
1	9	2	Polished Burl Walnut/Camphor	264,228	240,120
1	9	2	President Polished Ebony	216,040	196,511
1	9	2	President Polished Mahogany/Walnut	232,300	211,226
1	9	2	President Polished Bubinga	238,398	216,745
1	9	2	President Burl Walnut	277,016	251,693
1	9	2	Wilhelm II Satin and Polished Ebony	237,805	216,208
1	9	2	Wilhelm II Polished Mahogany/Walnut	256,830	233,425
1	9	2	Wilhelm II Polished Pyramid Mahogany	278,022	252,604
1	9	2	Wilhelm II Polished Burl Walnut	284,120	258,122
1	9	2	Ambassador Santos Rosewood	279,757	254,174
1	9	2	Ambassador Walnut	274,391	249,318
1	9	2	Nicolas II Satin Walnut with Burl Inlay	290,651	264,033
1	9	2	Jubilee Polished Ebony	223,144	202,940
1	9	2	Jubilee Polished Mahogany/Walnut	239,404	217,655
1	9	2	Dynasty	288,600	262,176

Model	Feet	Inches	Description	MSRP	SMP

BLÜTHNER (continued)

Model	Feet	Inches	Description	MSRP	SMP
1	9	2	Julius Bluthner Edition	230,798	209,867
1	9	2	Queen Victoria JB Edition Polished Rosewood	244,938	222,663
1	9	2	Crystal Edition Elegance	273,060	248,113
1	9	2	Crystal Edition Idyllic	316,350	287,290
Grands			e-volution Hybrid Piano System, add	8,800	7,964

BÖSENDORFER

Verticals

Model	Feet	Inches	Description	MSRP	SMP
130		52	Satin and Polished Ebony	76,999	72,998
130		52	Satin and Polished White, other colors	91,999	86,998
130		52	Polished, Satin, Open-pore: Walnut, Cherry, Mahogany, Pomele	98,999	92,998
130		52	Polished , Satin, Open-pore: Pyramid Mahogany, Burl Walnut, Birdseye Maple, Macassar, Madronna, Vavona, Wenge	103,999	98,998

Grands

Model	Feet	Inches	Description	MSRP	SMP
155	5	1	Satin and Polished Ebony	121,999	114,998
155	5	1	Satin and Polished White, other colors	136,999	128,998
155	5	1	Polished, Satin, Open-pore: Walnut, Cherry, Mahogany, Pomele	146,999	138,998
155	5	1	Polished , Satin, Open-pore: Pyramid Mahogany, Burl Walnut, Birdseye Maple, Macassar, Madronna, Vavona, Wenge	159,999	150,998
155	5	1	Chrome: Satin and Polished Ebony	138,999	130,998
170VC	5	7	Satin and Polished Ebony	126,999	120,998
170VC	5	7	Satin and Polished White, other colors	142,999	134,998
170VC	5	7	Polished, Satin, Open-pore: Walnut, Cherry, Mahogany, Pomele	153,999	144,998
170VC	5	7	Polished , Satin, Open-pore: Bubinga, Pyramid Mahogany, Santos Rosewood, Burl Walnut, Birdseye Maple, Macassar, Madronna, Vavona, Wenge	164,999	154,998
170VC	5	7	Chrome: Satin and Polished Ebony	142,999	134,998
170VC	5	7	Johann Strauss: Satin and Polished Ebony w/Maple	152,999	144,998
170VC	5	7	Johann Strauss: Any finish and veneer	178,999	168,998
170VC	5	7	Liszt: Polished Vavona	182,999	172,998
170VC	5	7	Chopin, Louis XVI: Satin Pommele	207,999	196,998
170VC	5	7	Baroque: Light Satin Ivory; Vienna: Polished Amboyna	232,999	218,998
170VC	5	7	Artisan Satin and Polished	297,999	280,998
185VC CS	6	1	Conservatory Satin Ebony	116,999	110,998
185VC	6	1	Satin and Polished Ebony	133,999	126,998
185VC	6	1	Satin and Polished White, other colors	149,999	140,998
185VC	6	1	Polished, Satin, Open-pore: Walnut, Cherry, Mahogany, Pomele	157,999	148,998
185VC	6	1	Polished , Satin, Open-pore: Pyramid Mahogany, Burl Walnut, Birdseye Maple, Macassar, Madronna, Vavona, Wenge	169,999	160,998

PIANOBUYER *Model & Price Supplement*

Model	Feet	Inches	Description	MSRP	SMP
BÖSENDORFER *(continued)*					
185VC	6	1	Chrome: Satin and Polished Ebony	149,999	140,998
185VC	6	1	Johann Strauss: Satin and Polished Ebony w/Maple	159,999	150,998
185VC	6	1	Johann Strauss: Any finish and veneer	185,000	174,998
185VC	6	1	Liszt: Polished Vavona	189,999	178,998
185VC	6	1	Edge: Satin and Polished Ebony	212,999	200,998
185VC	6	1	Chopin, Louis XVI: Satin Pommele	215,999	202,998
185VC	6	1	Baroque: Satin Light Ivory; Vienna: Polished Amboyna	236,999	222,998
185VC	6	1	Porsche Design: Diamond Black Metallic Gloss	248,999	234,998
185VC	6	1	Artisan Satin and Polished	306,999	288,998
200CS	6	7	Conservatory Satin Ebony	122,999	116,998
200	6	7	Satin and Polished Ebony	144,999	136,998
200	6	7	Satin and Polished White, other colors	161,999	152,998
200	6	7	Polished, Satin, Open-pore: Walnut, Cherry, Mahogany, Pomele	172,999	162,998
200	6	7	Polished , Satin, Open-pore: Pyramid Mahogany, Burl Walnut, Birdseye Maple, Macassar, Madronna, Vavona, Wenge	185,999	174,998
200	6	7	Chrome Satin and Polished Ebony	145,596	120,744
200	6	7	Chrome: Satin and Polished Ebony	159,999	150,998
200	6	7	Johann Strauss: Satin and Polished Ebony w/Maple	170,999	160,998
200	6	7	Johann Strauss: Any finish and veneer	201,999	190,998
200	6	7	Dragonfly: Maple and Polished Ebony	206,999	194,998
200	6	7	Liszt: Polished Vavona	206,999	194,998
200	6	7	Beethoven Polished Ebony, Klimt "Woman in Gold"	176,999	166,998
200	6	7	Beethoven: Chrome; Cocteau: White	204,999	192,998
200	6	7	Edge: Satin and Polished Ebony	233,999	220,998
200	6	7	Chopin, Louis XVI: Satin Pommele	236,999	222,998
200	6	7	Baroque: Satin Light Ivory; Vienna: Polished Amboyna	259,999	244,998
200	6	7	Artisan Satin and Polished	325,999	306,998
214VC CS	7		Conservatory Satin Ebony	132,999	126,998
214VC	7		Satin and Polished Ebony	158,999	150,998
214VC	7		Satin and Polished White, other colors	181,999	170,998
214VC	7		Polished, Satin, Open-pore: Walnut, Cherry, Mahogany, Pomele	193,999	182,998
214VC	7		Polished , Satin, Open-pore: Pyramid Mahogany, Burl Walnut, Birdseye Maple, Macassar, Madronna, Vavona, Wenge	211,999	198,998
214VC	7		Chrome: Satin and Polished Ebony	180,999	170,998
214VC	7		Johann Strauss: Satin and Polished Ebony w/Maple	189,999	178,998
214VC	7		Johann Strauss: Any finish and veneer	227,999	214,998
214VC	7		Liszt: Polished Vavona	233,999	220,998
214VC	7		Beethoven: Polished Ebony, Klimt "Woman in Gold"	191,999	182,998
214VC	7		Beethoven: Chrome; Cocteau: White	225,999	212,998
214VC	7		Edge: Satin and Polished Ebony	258,999	246,998
214VC	7		Chopin, Louis XVI: Satin Pommele	266,999	250,998
214VC	7		Baroque: Satin Light Ivory; Vienna: Polished Amboyna	292,999	274,998
214VC	7		Porsche Design: Diamond Black Metallic Gloss	308,999	290,998

Acoustic Piano Model & Pricing Guide

Model	Feet	Inches	Description	MSRP	SMP
BÖSENDORFER (continued)					
214VC	7		Audi Design Polished Ebony	372,999	352,998
214VC	7		Artisan Satin and Polished	372,999	352,998
225	7	4	Satin and Polished Ebony	178,999	168,998
225	7	4	Satin and Polished White, other colors	197,999	186,998
225	7	4	Polished, Satin, Open-pore: Walnut, Cherry, Mahogany, Pomele	212,999	200,998
225	7	4	Polished , Satin, Open-pore: Pyramid Mahogany, Burl Walnut, Birdseye Maple, Macassar, Madronna, Vavona, Wenge	229,999	216,998
225	7	4	Chrome: Satin and Polished Ebony	193,999	182,999
225	7	4	Johann Strauss: Satin and Polished Ebony w/Maple	204,999	192,998
225	7	4	Johann Strauss: Any finish and veneer	248,999	234,998
225	7	4	Liszt: Polished Vavona	255,999	240,998
225	7	4	Chopin, Louis XVI: Satin Pommele	291,999	274,998
225	7	4	Baroque: Satin Light Ivory; Vienna: Polished Amboyna	319,999	300,998
225	7	4	Artisan Satin and Polished	398,999	374,998
225	7	4	Grand Bohemian: Polished Ebony	420,000	420,000
280VC	9	2	Satin and Polished Ebony	229,999	216,998
280VC	9	2	Satin and Polished White, other colors	254,999	240,998
280VC	9	2	Polished, Satin, Open-pore: Walnut, Cherry, Mahogany, Pomele	274,999	258,998
280VC	9	2	Polished , Satin, Open-pore: Pyramid Mahogany, Burl Walnut, Birdseye Maple, Macassar, Madronna, Vavona, Wenge	297,999	280,998
280VC	9	2	Johann Strauss: Satin and Polished Ebony w/Maple	270,999	254,998
280VC	9	2	Johann Strauss: Any finish and veneer	323,999	304,998
280VC	9	2	Liszt: Polished Vavona	331,999	312,998
280VC	9	2	Chopin, Louis XVI: Satin Pommele	379,999	356,998
280VC	9	2	Baroque: Satin Light Ivory; Vienna: Polished Amboyna	412,999	390,998
280VC	9	2	Porsche Design: Diamond Black Metallic Gloss	437,999	412,998
280VC	9	2	Artisan Satin and Polished	472,999	444,998
290	9	6	Satin and Polished Ebony	262,999	246,998
290	9	6	Satin and Polished White, other colors	288,999	272,998
290	9	6	Polished, Satin, Open-pore: Walnut, Cherry, Mahogany, Pomele	312,999	294,998
290	9	6	Polished , Satin, Open-pore: Pyramid Mahogany, Burl Walnut, Birdseye Maple, Macassar, Madronna, Vavona, Wenge	338,999	318,998
290	9	6	Johann Strauss: Satin and Polished Ebony w/Maple	302,999	284,998
290	9	6	Johann Strauss: Any finish and veneer	369,999	346,998
290	9	6	Liszt: Polished Vavona	377,999	354,998
290	9	6	Chopin, Louis XVI: Satin Pommele	429,999	404,998
290	9	6	Baroque: Satin Light Ivory; Vienna: Polished Amboyna	472,999	444,998
290	9	6	Artisan Satin and Polished	536,999	506,998
Select models			Disklavier Enspire PRO, add	39,999	37,998

Model	Feet	Inches	Description	MSRP	SMP

BOSTON

Boston MSRP is the price at the New York retail store.

Verticals

Model	Feet	Inches	Description	MSRP	SMP
UP-118E PE		46	Satin and Polished Ebony	12,300	12,300
UP-118E PE		46	Polished Mahogany	14,200	14,200
UP-118E PE		46	Satin and Polished Walnut	14,200	14,200
UP-118S PE		46	Satin Black Oak	8,100	8,100
UP-120S PE-II		48	Polished Ebony	8,200	8,200
UP-120S PE-II		48	Satin Walnut	9,700	9,700
UP-126E PE		50	Polished Ebony	14,700	14,700
UP-126E PE		50	Polished Mahogany	17,100	17,100
UP-132E PE		52	Polished Ebony	16,400	16,400

Grands

Model	Feet	Inches	Description	MSRP	SMP
GP-156 PE-II	5	1	Satin and Polished Ebony	22,600	22,600
GP-163 PE-II	5	4	Satin and Polished Ebony	27,400	27,400
GP-163 PE-II	5	4	Satin and Polished Mahogany	30,100	30,100
GP-163 PE-II	5	4	Satin and Polished Walnut	30,400	30,400
GP-163 PE-II	5	4	Polished White	33,800	33,800
GP-178 PE-II	5	10	Satin and Polished Ebony	32,100	32,100
GP-178A PE-II	5	10	Polished Ebony with Silver Hardware	33,900	33,900
GP-178 PE-II	5	10	Satin and Polished Mahogany	34,600	34,600
GP-178 PE-II	5	10	Satin and Polished Walnut	35,100	35,100
GP-193 PE-II	6	4	Satin and Polished Ebony	41,700	41,700
GP-215 PE-II	7	1	Polished Ebony	54,500	54,500

BRODMANN

Verticals

Model	Feet	Inches	Description	MSRP	SMP
CE 118		47	Polished Ebony	10,290	6,580
PE 118V		47	Vienna Polished Ebony	13,990	8,580
PE 121		48	Polished Ebony	12,890	7,980
PE 121		48	Polished Mahogany/Walnut	13,990	8,580
PE 121		48	Polished White	14,390	8,780
PE 121		48	Polished Two Tone (Apple Tree Saphire/Ebony)	15,490	9,380
PE 124V		48	Vienna Polished Ebony	16,190	9,780
PE 124V		48	Vienna Polished Bubinga	17,290	10,380
PE 126I		49	Polished Ebony w/Institutional Wide Music Desk	15,790	9,580
PE 130		52	Polished Ebony	19,890	11,780
PE 132V		52	Vienna Polished Ebony	21,390	12,580
AS 132		52	Polished Ebony	29,490	16,980

Grands

Model	Feet	Inches	Description	MSRP	SMP
CE 148	4	10	Polished Ebony	25,390	14,780
CE 175	5	9	Polished Ebony	29,490	16,980
PE 150	5		Polished Ebony	30,190	17,380
PE 162	5	4	Polished Ebony	35,390	20,180

Model	Feet	Inches	Description	MSRP	SMP
BRODMANN (continued)					
PE 162	5	4	Polished Mahogany/Walnut/Walnut Burst	39,090	22,180
PE 162	5	4	Polished White	37,590	21,380
PE 162	5	4	Polished Bubinga	39,390	22,380
PE 162	5	4	Polished Two Tone (Ebony/Bubinga)	36,090	20,580
PE 162	5	4	Polished Two Tone (Apple Tree Saphire/Ebony)	39,090	22,180
PE 187	6	2	Polished Ebony	40,190	22,780
PE 187 V	6	2	Polished Ebony w/Carbon-Fiber Action	46,790	26,380
PE 187	6	2	Polished Mahogany/Walnut	43,890	24,780
PE 187	6	2	Polished White	43,090	24,380
PE 187	6	2	Polished Bubinga	45,290	25,580
PE 187	6	2	Strauss Polished Ebony	43,090	24,380
PE 187	6	2	Strauss Polished Two Tone (Ebony/Bubinga)	44,190	24,980
PE 212	7		Polished Ebony	63,390	35,380
PE 228	7	5	Polished Ebony	82,590	45,780
AS 188	6	2	Polished Ebony	66,990	45,660
AS 211	7		Polished Ebony	84,990	57,660
AS 227	7	6	Polished Ebony	96,990	65,660
AS 275	9		Polished Ebony	159,990	86,980
Grands			With Carbon-Fiber Action, add	6,600	3,600

CLINE
Verticals

Model	Feet	Inches	Description	MSRP	SMP
CL118		46.5	Polished Ebony		7,196
CL118		46.5	Polished Walnut/Mahogany		7,616
CL121/123		48	Polished Ebony		8,198
CL121/123		48	Polished Mahogany/Walnut		8,998

Grands

Model	Feet	Inches	Description	MSRP	SMP
CL 150	4	11	Polished Ebony		14,966

CRISTOFORI
Verticals

Model	Feet	Inches	Description	MSRP	SMP
V450		45	Polished Ebony	4,699	4,699
V450		45	Polished Mahogany	4,899	4,899
V465		46.5	Polished Ebony	4,999	4,999
V465		46.5	Polished Mahogany	5,199	5,199
V480LS		48	Polished Ebony	5,999	5,756
V480LS		48	Polished Mahogany	6,299	5,978

Grands

Model	Feet	Inches	Description	MSRP	SMP
G410L	4	10	Polished Ebony	9,990	9,786
G410L	4	10	Polished Mahogany	10,290	10,194
G53L	5	3	Satin Ebony	11,290	10,650

Model	Feet	Inches	Description	MSRP	SMP

CRISTOFORI *(continued)*

Model	Feet	Inches	Description	MSRP	SMP
G53L	5	3	Polished Ebony	10,990	10,242
G53L	5	3	Polished Mahogany/Snow White	11,290	10,650
G57L	5	7	Satin Ebony	12,790	12,232
G57L	5	7	Polished Ebony	12,490	11,838
G57L	5	7	Polished Mahogany	12,790	12,232
G62L	6	2	Satin Ebony	15,290	14,730
G62L	6	2	Polished Ebony	14,990	14,334

CUNNINGHAM

Verticals

Model	Inches	Description	MSRP	SMP
Studio Upright	48	Satin Ebony	9,890	9,890
Studio Upright	48	Polished Ebony	9,290	9,290
Studio Upright	48	Satin Mahogany	10,290	10,290
Studio Upright	48	Polished Mahogany	9,690	9,690

Grands

Model	Feet	Inches	Description	MSRP	SMP
Baby Grand	5		Satin Ebony	22,490	22,490
Baby Grand	5		Polished Ebony	21,290	21,290
Baby Grand	5		Satin Mahogany	23,190	23,190
Baby Grand	5		Polished Mahogany	21,990	21,990
Studio Grand	5	4	Satin Ebony	25,090	25,090
Studio Grand	5	4	Polished Ebony	23,890	23,890
Studio Grand	5	4	Satin Mahogany	25,790	25,790
Studio Grand	5	4	Polished Mahogany	24,590	24,590
Parlour Grand	5	10	Satin Ebony	30,490	30,490
Parlour Grand	5	10	Polished Ebony	29,290	29,290
Parlour Grand	5	10	Satin Mahogany	31,190	31,190
Parlour Grand	5	10	Polished Mahogany	29,990	29,990
Chamber Grand	7		Satin Ebony	46,290	46,290
Chamber Grand	7		Polished Ebony	44,790	44,790
Concert Grand	9		Satin Ebony	70,990	70,990
Concert Grand	9		Polished Ebony	68,990	68,990

DISKLAVIER — see Yamaha; see also Bösendorfer

EMERSON

Price includes adjustable leather-top bench.

Verticals

Model	Inches	Description	MSRP	SMP
EM8	51	Polished Ebony	28,559	17,320

Model	Feet	Inches	Description	MSRP	SMP

EMERSON *(continued)*
Grands

Model	Feet	Inches	Description	MSRP	SMP
EM168	5	6	Polished Ebony	72,434	42,390
EM180	5	11	Polished Ebony	85,805	50,032

ESSEX
Essex MSRP is the price at the New York retail store.
Verticals

Model	Inches	Description	MSRP	SMP
EUP-108C	42	Continental Polished Ebony	5,890	5,890
EUP-111E	44	Polished Ebony	6,590	6,590
EUP-111E	44	Polished Sapele Mahogany	6,990	6,700
EUP-116E	45	Polished Ebony	7,390	6,940
EUP-116E	45	Polished Sapele Mahogany	7,690	7,040
EUP-116E	45	Polished White	7,990	7,280
EUP-116CT	45	Contemporary Satin Lustre Sapele Mahogany	8,490	7,800
EUP-116QA	45	Queen Anne Satin Lustre Cherry	8,190	7,940
EUP-116EC	45	English Country Satin Lustre Walnut	8,190	7,760
EUP-116FF	45	Formal French Satin Lustre Brown Cherry	8,490	7,980
EUP-123E	48	Satin Ebony w/Chrome Hardware	8,890	8,180
EUP-123E	48	Polished Ebony	7,890	7,480
EUP-123E	48	Polished Ebony w/Chrome Hardware	7,990	7,600
EUP-123E	48	Polished Sapele Mahogany	8,990	8,000
EUP-123FL	48	Empire Satin Walnut	9,100	8,060
EUP-123FL	48	Empire Satin Sapele Mahogany	9,100	8,300
EUP-123S	48	Institutional Studio Polished Ebony	7,890	7,820

Grands

Model	Feet	Inches	Description	MSRP	SMP
EGP-155	5	1	Satin and Polished Ebony	14,300	14,300
EGP-155	5	1	Polished Sapele Mahogany	15,700	15,700
EGP-155	5	1	Polished White	19,200	16,940
EGP-155F	5	1	French Provincial Satin Lustre Brown Cherry	18,200	18,120
EGP-173	5	8	Polished Ebony	18,100	18,100

ESTONIA
The Estonia factory can make custom-designed finishes with exotic veneers; prices upon request.
Prices here include adjustable artist benches.
Grands

Model	Feet	Inches	Description	MSRP	SMP
L168	5	6	Polished Ebony	45,990	43,615
L168	5	6	Polished Mahogany/Walnut	49,749	46,873
L168	5	6	Polished Kewazinga Bubinga	53,965	50,992
L168	5	6	Polished Pyramid Mahogany	59,717	56,505
L168	6	7	Polished Palisander Rosewood	59,717	56,505
L168	5	6	Polished White	49,749	46,873
L168	5	6	Hidden Beauty Polished Ebony w/Bubinga	50,897	47,883
L190	6	3	Polished Ebony	56,478	53,021

Model	Feet	Inches	Description	MSRP	SMP

ESTONIA (continued)

Model	Feet	Inches	Description	MSRP	SMP
L190	6	3	Polished Mahogany/Walnut	60,163	56,923
L190	6	3	Polished Pyramid Mahogany	71,820	56,484
L190	6	3	Polished Palisander Rosewood	71,820	66,303
L190	6	3	Polished Kewazinga Bubinga	64,772	61,169
L190	6	3	Polished White	60,163	56,923
L190	6	3	Hidden Beauty Polished Ebony w/Bubinga	59,399	56,069
L210	6	10	Polished Ebony	66,465	63,836
L210	6	10	Polished Mahogany/Walnut/White	73,112	70,117
L210	6	10	Polished Pyramid Mahogany	83,081	79,533
L210	6	10	Polished Kewazinga Bubinga	78,435	75,138
L210	6	10	Polished Palisander Rosewood	83,081	79,533
L210	6	10	Hidden Beauty Polished Ebony w/Bubinga	70,592	67,508
L225	7	4	Polished Ebony	83,673	78,012
L225	7	4	Polished Mahogany/Walnut/White	90,013	84,700
L225	7	4	Polished Pyramid Mahogany	99,914	95,246
L225	7	4	Polished Kewazinga Bubinga	90,405	87,777
L225	7	4	Polished Palisander Rosewood	99,914	95,246
L225	7	4	Hidden Beauty Polished Ebony w/Bubinga	88,867	83,424
L274	9		Polished Ebony	133,497	118,312
L274	9		Polished Mahogany/Walnut	146,402	130,699
L274	9		Polished Pyramid Mahogany	151,467	144,390
L274	9		Polished White	137,736	125,153

FANDRICH & SONS

These are the prices on the Fandrich & Sons website. Other finishes available at additional cost. See website for details.

Verticals

Model		Inches	Description	MSRP	SMP
EU131-V		52	Polished Ebony	12,990	12,990

Grands

Model	Feet	Inches	Description	MSRP	SMP
160-S	5	3	Polished Ebony	14,650	14,650
170-S	5	7	Polished Ebony	16,995	16,995
212-E	7		Polished Ebony	28,650	28,650

FAZIOLI

Fazioli is willing to make custom-designed cases with exotic veneers, marquetry, and other embellishments. Prices on request to Fazioli.

Grands

Model	Feet	Inches	Description	MSRP	SMP
F156	5	2	Satin and Polished Ebony	123,000	116,850
F156	5	2	Satin and Polished White/Red	141,500	134,425
F156	5	2	Satin and Polished Walnut/Cherry/Mahogany	153,800	146,110
F156	5	2	Satin and Polished Pyramid Mahogany/Macassar	172,200	163,590
F156	5	2	Satin and Polished Briers: Mahogany/California Walnut/ Sequoia	184,500	175,275
F156	5	2	Satin and Polished Olive	196,200	186,390

Model	Feet	Inches	Description	MSRP	SMP
FAZIOLI *(continued)*					
F183	6		Satin and Polished Ebony	126,700	120,365
F183	6		Satin and Polished White/Red	144,100	136,895
F183	6		Satin and Polished Walnut/Cherry/Mahogany	156,700	148,865
F183	6		Satin and Polished Pyramid Mahogany/Macassar	175,500	166,725
F183	6		Satin and Polished Briers: Mahogany/California Walnut/ Sequoia	188,000	178,600
F183	6		Satin and Polished Olive	199,200	189,240
F212	7		Satin and Polished Ebony	145,800	138,510
F212	7		Satin and Polished White/Red	157,100	149,245
F212	7		Satin and Polished Walnut/Cherry/Mahogany	171,400	162,830
F212	7		Satin and Polished Pyramid Mahogany/Macassar	185,700	176,415
F212	7		Satin and Polished Briers: Mahogany/California Walnut/ Sequoia	200,000	190,000
F212	7		Satin and Polished Olive	211,900	201,305
F228	7	6	Satin and Polished Ebony	166,200	157,890
F228	7	6	Satin and Polished White/Red	179,200	170,240
F228	7	6	Satin and Polished Walnut/Cherry/Mahogany	195,500	185,725
F228	7	6	Satin and Polished Pyramid Mahogany/Macassar	211,900	201,305
F228	7	6	Satin and Polished Briers: Mahogany/California Walnut/ Sequoia	228,100	216,695
F228	7	6	Satin and Polished Olive	254,800	242,060
F278	9	2	Satin and Polished Ebony	225,100	213,845
F278	9	2	Satin and Polished White/Red	240,400	228,380
F278	9	2	Satin and Polished Walnut/Cherry/Mahogany	262,300	249,185
F278	9	2	Satin and Polished Pyramid Mahogany/Macassar	284,100	269,895
F278	9	2	Satin and Polished Briers: Mahogany/California Walnut/ Sequoia	306,000	290,700
F278	9	2	Satin and Polished Olive	326,100	309,795
F308	10	2	Satin and Polished Ebony	245,700	233,415
F308	10	2	Satin and Polished White/Red	262,400	249,280
F308	10	2	Satin and Polished Walnut/Cherry/Mahogany	286,200	271,890
F308	10	2	Satin and Polished Pyramid Mahogany/Macassar	310,100	294,595
F308	10	2	Satin and Polished Briers: Mahogany/California Walnut/ Sequoia	333,800	317,110
F308	10	2	Satin and Polished Olive	347,000	329,650

FÖRSTER, AUGUST

Prices do not include bench. Euro = $1.22

Verticals

Model		Feet Inches	Description	MSRP	SMP
116 C		46	Chippendale Polished Ebony		36,700
116 C		46	Chippendale Polished Mahogany/Walnut		39,000
116 C		46	Chippendale Satin Ebony w/Carvings		34,500
116 C		46	Chippendale Satin Mahogany/Walnut w/Carvings		36,500
116 D		46	Continental Satin Ebony		24,400
116 D		46	Continental Polished Ebony		26,800
116 D		46	Continental Satin Mahogany/Walnut/Oak/Cherry		26,600

Model	Feet	Inches	Description	MSRP	SMP
FÖRSTER, AUGUST *(continued)*					
116 D		46	Continental Polished Mahogany/Walnut/Oak/Cherry		29,200
116 D		46	Continental Satin Beech		24,380
116 D		46	Continental Polished White with bench		29,000
116 E		46	Satin Ebony		28,800
116 E		46	Polished Ebony		31,100
116 E		46	Satin Mahogany/Walnut/Oak/Cherry		30,900
116 E		46	Polished Mahogany/Walnut/Oak/Cherry		33,400
116 E		46	Satin Beech		29,200
116 E		46	Polished White with bench		33,200
125 F		49	Polished Ebony		35,600
125 G		49	Satin Ebony		32,600
125 G		49	Polished Ebony		34,900
125 G		49	Satin Mahogany/Walnut/Oak/Cherry		35,300
125 G		49	Polished Mahogany/Walnut/Oak/Cherry		38,000
125 G		49	Satin Beech		33,000
125 G		49	Polished White with bench		37,500
125 G		49	With Oval Medallion, add		1,600
134 K		53	Polished Ebony		53,200
Grands					
170	5	8	Satin Ebony		67,400
170	5	8	Polished Ebony		72,000
170	5	8	Satin Mahogany/Walnut/Cherry		71,800
170	5	8	Polished Mahogany/Walnut/Cherry		76,100
170	5	8	Polished White with bench		77,600
170	5	8	Chippendale Satin Walnut		116,800
170	5	8	Antik Satin Walnut		140,600
170	5	8	Classik Polished Ebony		82,200
170	5	8	Classik Polished Mahogany/Walnut		94,200
170	5	8	Classik Polished White with bench		87,800
190	6	4	Satin Ebony		76,200
190	6	4	Polished Ebony		80,900
190	6	4	Satin Mahogany/Walnut/Cherry		80,400
190	6	4	Polished Mahogany/Walnut/Cherry		84,800
190	6	4	Polished White with bench		86,400
190	6	4	Chippendale Satin Walnut		125,500
190	6	4	Antik Satin Walnut		157,900
190	6	4	Classik Polished Ebony		90,900
190	6	4	Classik Polished Mahogany/Walnut		106,000
190	6	4	Classik Polished White with bench		96,600
190	6	4	Rokoko Polished White with bench		250,000
215	7	2	Polished Ebony		96,500
215	7	2	Satin Mahogany/Walnut/Cherry		101,400
215	7	2	Polished Mahogany/Walnut/Cherry		105,600
215	7	2	Polished White with bench		107,200
275	9	1	Polished Ebony		172,000
275	9	1	Polished White with bench		183,000

Model	Feet	Inches	Description	MSRP	SMP

GEYER, A.

Verticals

Model	Feet	Inches	Description	MSRP	SMP
GU 115		45	Polished Ebony	6,185	4,990
GU 115		45	Polished Mahogany/Walnut	6,685	5,290
GU 115		45	Polished White	6,485	5,190
GU 123		47	Polished Ebony	6,785	5,390
GU 123		47	Polished Mahogany/Walnut	7,235	5,690
GU 123		47	Polished White	7,085	5,590
GU 133		52	Polished Ebony	7,685	5,990
GU 133		52	Polished Mahogany/Walnut	8,285	6,390
GU 133		52	Polished White	7,985	6,190

Grands

Model	Feet	Inches	Description	MSRP	SMP
GG 150	4	11	Polished Ebony	12,785	9,590
GG 150	4	11	Polished Mahogany/Walnut	13,685	9,990
GG 150	4	11	Polished White	13,235	9,870
GG 160	5	3	Polished Ebony	14,535	10,590
GG 160	5	3	Polished Mahogany/Walnut	15,285	10,990
GG 160	5	3	Polished White	15,035	10,890
GG 170	5	7	Polished Ebony	16,385	11,790
GG 170	5	7	Polished Mahogany/Walnut	16,715	12,010
GG 170	5	7	Polished White	16,835	12,090
GG 185	6	1	Polished Ebony	18,785	13,390
GG 185	6	1	Polished Mahogany/Walnut	19,585	13,990
GG 185	6	1	Polished White	19,385	13,790
GG 230	7	7	Polished Ebony	29,225	25,990

GROTRIAN

Sostenuto included with Grotrian vertical models G-124 and G-132, and all Grotrian grand models.

Grotrian Verticals

Model	Feet	Inches	Description	MSRP	SMP
Concerto G-124		49	Polished Ebony	53,700	36,800
Concerto G-132		52	Polished Ebony	68,700	46,800

Wilhelm Grotrian Verticals

Model	Feet	Inches	Description	MSRP	SMP
WG-18		46.5	Polished Ebony	14,370	10,580
WG-23		48.5	Polished Ebony	16,230	11,820
WG-26		49.5	Polished Ebony	17,790	12,860
WG-32		52	Polished Ebony	20,610	14,740

Wilhelm Grotrian Studio Verticals

Model	Feet	Inches	Description	MSRP	SMP
WGS-116		46	Polished Ebony	9,360	7,240
WGS-120		47	Polished Ebony	10,620	8,080
WGS-122		48	Polished Ebony	11,880	8,920
WGS-125		49	Polished Ebony	13,110	9,740

Grotrian Grands

Model	Feet	Inches	Description	MSRP	SMP
Concerto G-165	5	5	(Chambre) Polished Ebony	103,500	70,000
Concerto G-192	6	3	(Cabinet) Polished Ebony	124,500	84,000

Model	Feet	Inches	Description	MSRP	SMP
GROTRIAN *(continued)*					
Concerto G-208	6	10	(Charis) Polished Ebony	133,500	90,000
Concerto G-225	7	4	(Concert) Polished Ebony	179,970	120,980
Concerto G-277	9	1	(Concert Royal) Polished Ebony	233,700	156,800
Wilhelm Grotrian Studio Grands					
WGS-152	5		Polished Ebony	24,780	17,520
WGS-165	5	5	Polished Ebony	29,790	20,860

HAESSLER

Prices do not include bench.

Verticals

Model		Inches	Description	MSRP	SMP
H 118		47	Polished Ebony	25,256	23,753
H 118		47	Satin Mahogany/Walnut	26,429	24,810
H 118		47	Polished Mahogany/Walnut	30,654	28,616
H 118		47	Satin Cherry	26,868	25,205
H 118		47	Polished Cherry	31,123	29,039
H 118		47	Satin Oak/Beech	25,067	23,583
H 118		47	Polished White	27,602	25,867
H 118		47	Polished Bubinga	31,358	29,250
H 118		47	Satin Mahogany w/Vavona Inlay	28,306	26,501
H 118		47	Polished Mahogany w/Vavona Inlay	32,062	29,885
H 118		47	Polished Burl Walnut	31,827	29,673
H 118		47	Satin Burl Walnut w/Walnut Inlay	28,306	26,501
H 118		47	Polished Burl Walnut w/Walnut Inlay	32,062	29,885
H 118		47	Satin Cherry and Yew	28,400	26,586
H 118		47	Polished Cherry and Yew	32,062	29,885
H 124		49	Polished Ebony	27,602	25,867
H 124		49	Satin Mahogany/Walnut	28,635	26,797
H 124		49	Polished Mahogany/Walnut	33,000	30,730
H 124		49	Satin Cherry	28,775	26,923
H 124		49	Polished Cherry	33,470	31,153
H 124		49	Satin Oak/Beech	28,541	26,713
H 124		49	Polished White	29,949	27,981
H 124		49	Polished Bubinga	33,705	31,365
H 124		49	Polished Pyramid Mahogany	37,320	34,622
H 124		49	Satin Mahogany w/Vavona Inlay	30,184	28,193
H 124		49	Polished Mahogany w/Vavona Inlay	35,583	33,057
H 124		49	Polished Burl Walnut	36,850	34,198
H 124		49	Satin Burl Walnut w/Walnut Inlay	30,184	28,193
H 124		49	Polished Burl Walnut w/Walnut Inlay	35,583	33,057
H 124		49	Satin Cherry and Yew	30,184	28,193
H 124		49	Polished Cherry and Yew	36,850	34,198
K 124		49	Polished Ebony	29,856	27,897
K 124		49	Satin Mahogany/Walnut	30,888	28,827
K 124		49	Polished Mahogany/Walnut	35,255	32,761

Model	Feet	Inches	Description	MSRP	SMP
HAESSLER *(continued)*					
K 124		49	Satin Cherry	31,030	28,955
K 124		49	Polished Cherry	35,724	33,184
K 124		49	Satin Oak/Beech	30,795	28,743
K 124		49	Polished White	32,266	30,068
K 124		49	Polished Bubinga	35,959	33,395
K 124		49	Polished Pyramid Mahogany	39,573	36,651
K 124		49	Satin Mahogany w/Vavona Inlay	32,438	30,223
K 124		49	Polished Mahogany w/Vavona Inlay	37,836	35,086
K 124		49	Polished Burl Walnut	39,104	36,229
K 124		49	Satin Burl Walnut w/Walnut Inlay	32,438	30,223
K 124		49	Polished Burl Walnut w/Walnut Inlay	37,836	35,086
K 124		49	Satin Cherry and Yew	32,438	30,223
K 124		49	Polished Cherry and Yew	39,104	36,229
H 132		52	Polished Ebony	30,888	28,827
H 132		52	Satin Mahogany/Walnut	31,358	29,250
H 132		52	Polished Mahogany/Walnut	36,052	33,479
H 132		52	Satin Cherry	32,766	30,519
H 132		52	Polished Cherry	36,522	33,903
H 132		52	Polished White	33,235	30,941
H 132		52	Polished Bubinga	36,991	34,325
H 132		52	Palisander Rosewood	39,104	36,229
H 132		52	Polished Pyramid Mahogany	40,042	37,074
H 132		52	Satin Mahogany w/Vavona Inlay	34,409	31,999
H 132		52	Polished Mahogany w/Vavona Inlay	39,104	36,229
H 132		52	Polished Burl Walnut	40,104	37,130
H 132		52	Satin Burl Walnut w/Walnut Inlay	34,409	31,999
H 132		52	Polished Burl Walnut w/Walnut Inlay	39,104	36,229
H 132		52	Satin Cherry and Yew	34,409	31,999
H 132		52	Polished Cherry and Yew	40,104	37,130
K 132		52	Polished Ebony	34,034	31,661
K 132		52	Satin Mahogany/Walnut	34,504	32,085
K 132		52	Polished Mahogany/Walnut	39,198	36,314
K 132		52	Satin Cherry	35,912	33,353
K 132		52	Polished Cherry	39,668	36,737
K 132		52	Polished White	36,381	33,776
K 132		52	Polished Bubinga	40,137	37,159
K 132		52	Palisander Rosewood	42,249	39,062
K 132		52	Polished Pyramid Mahogany	43,187	39,907
K 132		52	Satin Mahogany w/Vavona Inlay	37,555	34,833
K 132		52	Polished Mahogany w/Vavona Inlay	42,249	39,062
K 132		52	Polished Burl Walnut	42,249	39,062
K 132		52	Satin Burl Walnut w/Walnut Inlay	37,555	34,833
K 132		52	Polished Burl Walnut w/Walnut Inlay	42,249	39,062
K 132		52	Satin Cherry and Yew	37,555	34,833
K 132		52	Polished Cherry and Yew	42,249	39,062

Model	Feet	Inches	Description	MSRP	SMP

HAESSLER (continued)

Grands

Model	Feet	Inches	Description	MSRP	SMP
H 175	5	8	Polished Ebony	80,195	73,248
H 175	5	8	Satin Mahogany/Walnut	86,210	78,667
H 175	5	8	Polished Mahogany/Walnut	94,310	85,964
H 175	5	8	Satin Cherry	85,488	78,016
H 175	5	8	Polished Cherry	96,516	87,951
H 175	5	8	Polished White	85,809	78,305
H 175	5	8	Polished Bubinga	98,281	89,541
H 175	5	8	Palisander Rosewood	103,133	93,913
H 175	5	8	Polished Pyramid Mahogany	107,985	98,284
H 175	5	8	Polished Mahogany w/Vavona Inlay	118,131	107,424
H 175	5	8	Polished Burl Walnut	105,338	95,899
H 175	5	8	Polished Burl Walnut w/Walnut Inlay	118,131	107,424
H 175	5	8	Satin Cherry and Yew	111,955	101,860
H 175	5	8	Polished Cherry and Yew	118,131	107,424
H 175	5	8	Classic Alexandra Polished Ebony	95,413	86,958
H 175	5	8	Classic Alexandra Polished Walnut	109,122	99,308
H 175	5	8	Classic Alexandra Burl Walnut	120,042	109,146
H 175	5	8	Classic Alexandra Palisander	117,858	107,178
H 175	5	8	Louis XIV Satin White w/Gold	152,892	138,741
H 175	5	8	Satin and Polished Louis XV Mahogany	116,984	106,391
H 175	5	8	Ambassador Palisander	144,155	130,869
H 175	5	8	Ambassador Walnut	139,786	126,933
H 186	6	1	Polished Ebony	85,047	77,619
H 186	6	1	Satin Mahogany/Walnut	91,426	83,366
H 186	6	1	Polished Mahogany/Walnut	99,162	90,335
H 186	6	1	Satin Cherry	90,340	82,387
H 186	6	1	Polished Cherry	101,368	92,323
H 186	6	1	Polished White	91,000	82,982
H 186	6	1	Polished Bubinga	105,780	96,297
H 186	6	1	Palisander Rosewood	107,985	98,284
H 186	6	1	Polished Pyramid Mahogany	114,602	104,245
H 186	6	1	Polished Mahogany w/Vavona Inlay	122,984	111,796
H 186	6	1	Polished Burl Walnut	110,190	100,270
H 186	6	1	Polished Burl Walnut w/Walnut Inlay	122,984	111,796
H 186	6	1	Satin Cherry and Yew	107,103	97,489
H 186	6	1	Polished Cherry and Yew	122,984	111,796
H 186	6	1	Classic Alexandra Polished Ebony	99,978	91,070
H 186	6	1	Classic Alexandra Polished Walnut	113,926	103,636
H 186	6	1	Classic Alexandra Burl Walnut	124,847	113,475
H 186	6	1	Classic Alexandra Palisander	122,663	111,507
H 186	6	1	Louis XIV Satin White w/Gold	157,260	142,676
H 186	6	1	Satin and Polished Louis XV Mahogany	121,789	110,720
H 186	6	1	Ambassador Palisander	157,260	142,676
H 186	6	1	Ambassador Walnut	152,892	138,741

Model	Feet	Inches	Description	MSRP	SMP
HAESSLER *(continued)*					
H 210	6	10	Polished Ebony	99,030	90,216
H 210	6	10	Satin Mahogany/Walnut	106,458	96,908
H 210	6	10	Polished Mahogany/Walnut	117,160	106,550
H 210	6	10	Satin Cherry	107,632	97,966
H 210	6	10	Polished Cherry	119,012	108,218
H 210	6	10	Polished White	105,962	96,461
H 210	6	10	Polished Bubinga	120,778	109,809
H 210	6	10	Palisander Rosewood	130,040	118,153
H 210	6	10	Polished Pyramid Mahogany	136,658	124,115
H 210	6	10	Polished Mahogany w/Vavona Inlay	145,480	132,063
H 210	6	10	Polished Burl Walnut	127,835	116,167
H 210	6	10	Polished Burl Walnut w/Walnut Inlay	145,480	132,063
H 210	6	10	Satin Cherry and Yew	127,924	116,247
H 210	6	10	Polished Cherry and Yew	145,480	132,063
H 210	6	10	Classic Alexandra Polished Ebony	113,796	103,519
H 210	6	10	Classic Alexandra Polished Walnut	131,749	119,693
H 210	6	10	Classic Alexandra Burl Walnut	142,320	129,216
H 210	6	10	Classic Alexandra Palisander	144,505	131,185
H 210	6	10	Louis XIV Satin White w/Gold	192,207	174,159
H 210	6	10	Satin and Polished Louis XV Mahogany	135,637	123,195
H 210	6	10	Ambassador Palisander	170,365	154,482
H 210	6	10	Ambassador Walnut	165,997	150,547

HAILUN

Verticals

Model	Feet	Inches	Description	MSRP	SMP
HU120		47.5	Polished Ebony	15,901	10,086
HU121		48	Polished Ebony	16,657	10,518
HU121		48	Polished Mahogany/Walnut	17,735	11,134
HU121		48	Chippendale Polished Mahogany/Walnut	18,225	11,414
HU1P		48	Polished Ebony	19,579	12,188
HU1EP		48	Polished Ebony w/Mahogany Accents	21,109	13,062
HU1EP		48	iPiano Hybrid, Polished Ebony w/Mahogany Accents	40,177	23,958
HU1EP		48	iPiano Hybrid, Polished White	40,177	23,958
HU5P		50	Polished Ebony	24,255	14,860
HU5P		50	Polished Ebony with Nickel Trim	25,064	15,322
HU5P		50	Polished Mahogany	25,064	15,322
HU7P		52	Polished Ebony w/Sostenuto	30,587	18,478

Grands

Model	Feet	Inches	Description	MSRP	SMP
HG150	4	10	Andante Polished Ebony	35,060	21,034
HG151	4	11.5	Polished Ebony	42,042	25,024
HG151	4	11.5	Polished Mahogany/Walnut/White	44,097	26,198
HG151C	4	11.5	Chippendale Polished Mahogany/Walnut	34,265	26,480
HG161	5	4	Polished Ebony	46,281	27,446
HG161	5	4	Polished Mahogany/Walnut/White	48,486	28,706
HG161G	5	4	Georgian Polished Mahogany/Walnut	37,730	29,154

Model	Feet	Inches	Description	MSRP	SMP

HAILUN *(continued)*

HG178	5	10	Polished Ebony	56,326	33,186
HG178	5	10	Polished Mahogany/Walnut/White	58,797	34,598
HG178B	5	10	Baroque Polished Ebony w/Birds-Eye Maple Accents	46,200	36,000
HG198	6	5	Emerson Polished Ebony	81,515	47,580
HG198	6	5	Emerson Polished Mahogany/Walnut/White	83,297	48,598
HG218	7	2	Paulello Polished Ebony	110,887	64,364

HALLET, DAVIS & CO.
Heritage Collection Verticals

H108		43	Continental Polished Ebony	5,295	4,300
H117H		46	Polished Ebony	5,950	4,500
H117H		46	Polished Mahogany	6,150	4,590
H118F		46	Demi-Chippendale Polished Ebony	5,995	4,700
H118F		46	Demi-Chippendale Polished Mahogany	6,195	4,790

Signature Collection Verticals

HS109D		43	Continental Polished Ebony	5,895	4,700
HS109D		43	Continental Polished Mahogany	6,195	4,900
HS115M2		45	Classic Studio Polished Ebony	7,395	4,990
HS115M2		45	Classic Studio Polished Mahogany/Walnut/White	7,595	5,190
HS118M		46.5	Polished Ebony	7,795	5,390
HS118M		46.5	Polished Mahogany/Walnut/White	7,995	5,590
HS121S		48	Polished Ebony	8,995	5,790
HS121S		48	Polished Mahogany/Walnut/White	9,295	5,990
HS131Y		52	Polished Ebony	9,895	6,790

Heritage Collection Grands

H142C	4	7	Polished Ebony	13,195	9,390

Signature Collection Grands

HS148	4	10	Satin Ebony	15,695	10,390
HS148	4	10	Polished Ebony	14,995	9,790
HS148	4	10	Polished Ebony w/Silver Plate	15,695	10,390
HS148	4	10	Polished Mahogany/Walnut/White	15,695	10,390
HS148	4	10	Polished White w/Silver Plate	16,495	10,990
HS160	5	3	Satin Ebony	16,995	11,590
HS160	5	3	Polished Ebony	16,495	10,990
HS160	5	3	Polished Ebony w/Silver Plate	16,995	11,590
HS160	5	3	Polished Mahogany/Walnut/White	16,995	11,590
HS170	5	7	Satin Ebony	17,995	12,790
HS170	5	7	Polished Ebony	17,495	12,190
HS170	5	7	Polished Mahogany/Walnut/White	17,995	12,790
HS188	6	2	Satin Ebony	20,995	15,390
HS188	6	2	Polished Ebony	20,495	14,790
HS188	6	2	Polished Mahogany/Walnut	20,995	15,390
HS212	7		Polished Ebony	29,995	28,990

Model	Feet	Inches	Description	MSRP	SMP

HARDMAN, PECK & CO.
Performance Series Verticals

Model	Feet	Inches	Description	MSRP	SMP
R110S		44	Polished Ebony	5,495	4,310
R110S		44	Polished Mahogany	5,695	4,390
R115LS		45	Polished Ebony	5,995	4,510
R115LS		45	Polished Mahogany	6,195	4,590
R116		46	School Polished Ebony	6,695	4,990
R116		46	School Satin Cherry	6,895	5,110
R117XK		46	Chippendale Polished Mahogany	6,695	4,910
R120LS		48	Polished Ebony	6,495	4,910
R120LS		48	Polished Mahogany	6,695	4,990
R132HA		52	Polished Ebony	9,495	6,490

Concert Series Verticals

Model	Feet	Inches	Description	MSRP	SMP
R110C		44	Polished Ebony	5,795	4,590
R110C		44	Polished Mahogany	5,995	4,790
R115GC		45	Polished Ebony	6,595	4,790
R115GC		45	Polished Mahogany	6,995	4,990
R123C		49	Polished Ebony	7,295	5,390
R123C		49	Polished Mahogany	7,595	5,590

Performance Series Grands

Model	Feet	Inches	Description	MSRP	SMP
R143S	4	8	Polished Ebony	13,895	9,390
R143S	4	8	Polished Mahogany	14,995	9,790
R143F	4	8	French Provincial Polished Mahogany	15,395	10,190
R150S	5		Polished Ebony	15,995	9,990
R158S	5	3	Polished Ebony	16,795	10,590
R158S	5	3	Polished Mahogany	17,495	10,990
R168S	5	7	Polished Ebony	18,195	11,390
R168S	5	7	Polished Mahogany	18,995	11,790
R185S	6	1	Polished Ebony	20,995	13,190
R185S	6	1	Polished Mahogany	22,395	13,790

Concert Series Grands

Model	Feet	Inches	Description	MSRP	SMP
R146C	4	10	Polished Ebony	14,595	9,390
R146C	4	10	Polished Mahogany	15,395	9,990
R165C	5	5	Polished Ebony	18,495	11,390
R165C	5	5	Polished Mahogany	19,495	11,990

HEINTZMAN & CO.
Heintzman Verticals

Model	Feet	Inches	Description	MSRP	SMP
121DL		48	Satin Mahogany	7,995	7,380
123B		48.5	Polished Mahogany	8,795	7,580
123F		48.5	French Provincial Polished Mahogany	7,995	6,980
126C		50	Polished Ebony	8,795	7,600

Model	Feet	Inches	Description	MSRP	SMP

HEINTZMAN & CO. *(continued)*

Model	Feet	Inches	Description	MSRP	SMP
126 Royal		50	Polished Ebony	9,795	8,200
132D		52	Polished Mahogany, Decorative Panel	11,795	8,980
132E		52	French Provincial Polished Ebony	11,795	8,780
132E		52	French Provincial Satin and Polished Mahogany	11,795	8,980
132 Royal		52	Satin Mahogany	12,795	9,580
140CK		55	Polished Mahogany	14,995	10,980

Gerhard Heintzman Verticals

Model	Feet	Inches	Description	MSRP	SMP
G118		47	Polished Ebony w/Silver Plate and Trim	4,995	4,995
G118		47	Polished Mahogany w/Silver Plate and Trim	5,195	5,195
G120		48	Polished Ebony w/Silver Plate and Trim	5,995	5,700
G120		48	Polished Mahogany w/Silver Plate and Trim	6,195	5,900
G126		50	Polished Ebony w/Silver Plate and Trim	7,995	6,400
G126		50	Polished Mahogany w/Silver Plate and Trim	8,195	6,600
G132		52	Polished Ebony w/Silver Plate and Trim	9,295	7,200

Heintzman Grands

Model	Feet	Inches	Description	MSRP	SMP
168	5	6	Polished Ebony	18,995	16,990
168	5	6	Polished Mahogany	19,995	17,390
168 Royal	5	6	Polished Ebony	23,995	17,990
186	6	1	Polished Ebony	21,995	18,980
186	6	1	Polished Mahogany	22,995	20,180
186 Royal	6	1	Polished Ebony	26,995	19,980
203	6	8	Polished Ebony	24,995	20,580
203 Royal	6	8	Polished Ebony	29,995	21,580
277	9		Polished Ebony	89,995	60,995

Gerhard Heintzman Grands

Model	Feet	Inches	Description	MSRP	SMP
G152	5		Polished Ebony	9,995	9,995
G152	5		Polished White	11,995	11,995
G152R	5		Empire Polished Mahogany	11,995	11,995
G168	5	6	Polished Ebony	15,995	12,800
G168	5	6	Polished White	19,995	13,800
G168R	5	6	Empire Polished Mahogany	17,995	13,800

HOFFMANN, W.

Vision Series Verticals

Model	Feet	Inches	Description	MSRP	SMP
V112		44.5	Polished Ebony	12,500	12,142
V112		44.5	Polished Mahogany/Walnut	15,900	15,044
V112		44.5	Polished White	14,900	13,593
V112		44.5	Chippendale Polished Mahogany	16,500	16,205
V112		44.5	Chippendale Polished Walnut	16,500	16,205
V120		47.6	Polished Ebony	13,500	12,868
V120		47.6	Polished Mahogany/Walnut	16,500	16,044

Model	Feet	Inches	Description	MSRP	SMP

HOFFMANN, W. *(continued)*

Model	Feet	Inches	Description	MSRP	SMP
V120		47.6	Polished White	15,500	15,044
V120		47.6	Chippendale Polished Mahogany	17,900	17,656
V120		47.6	Chippendale Polished Walnut	17,900	17,656
V120		47.6	Rococo Satin White	19,900	18,381
V120		47.6	Rococo Satin White w/Gold Painting	19,900	18,381
V126		49.6	Polished Ebony	14,900	14,319
V126		49.6	Polished White	17,900	16,495
V131		51.8	Polished Ebony	16,900	15,770

Tradition Series Verticals

Model	Feet	Inches	Description	MSRP	SMP
T122		48	Polished Ebony	16,900	16,044
T122		48	Satin Mahogany/Walnut	19,900	19,672
T122		48	Polished Mahogany/Walnut	19,900	19,672
T122		48	Polished White	18,900	18,221
T128		50.4	Polished Ebony	17,900	17,495
T128		50.4	Satin Mahogany/Walnut	21,900	21,123
T128		50.4	Polished Mahogany/Walnut	21,900	21,123
T128		50.4	Polished White	20,900	19,672

Professional Series Verticals

Model	Feet	Inches	Description	MSRP	SMP
P114		45	Polished Ebony w/Chrome Hardware	17,900	17,495
P114		45	Polished White w/Chrome Hardware	19,900	19,672
P120		47.2	Polished Ebony w/Chrome Hardware	18,900	18,801
P120		47.2	Polished White w/Chrome Hardware	20,900	20,793
P126		49.6	Polished Ebony w/Chrome Hardware	20,500	20,397

Vision Series Grands

Model	Feet	Inches	Description	MSRP	SMP
V158	5	2	Polished Ebony	29,900	29,247
V158	5	2	Polished Mahogany/Walnut	34,900	33,600
V158	5	2	Polished White	33,900	33,149
V175	5	9	Polished Ebony	32,900	32,423
V175	5	9	Polished Walnut/Mahogany	37,900	36,776
V175	5	9	Polished White	36,900	36,325
V183	6		Polished Ebony	35,900	35,325
V183	6		Polished Walnut/Mahogany	40,900	39,678
V183	6		Polished White	39,900	39,227

Tradition Series Grands

Model	Feet	Inches	Description	MSRP	SMP
T161	5	3	Polished Ebony	41,900	41,885
T161	5	3	Polished Mahogany/Walnut	47,900	46,870
T161	5	3	Polished White	46,900	46,313
T177	5	10	Polished Ebony	47,900	45,313
T177	5	10	Polished Mahogany/Walnut	52,900	49,983
T177	5	10	Polished White	51,900	49,426
T186	6	1	Polished Ebony	52,900	51,539
T186	6	1	Polished Mahogany/Walnut	57,900	56,209
T186	6	1	Polished White	56,900	55,652

Model	Feet	Inches	Description	MSRP	SMP

HOFFMANN, W. *(continued)*
Professional Series Grands

Model	Feet	Inches	Description	MSRP	SMP
P162	5	4	Polished Ebony w/Chrome Hardware	52,900	50,916
P188	6	2	Polished Ebony w/Chrome Hardware	57,900	55,586
P206	6	9	Polished Ebony w/Chrome Hardware	64,900	61,812

HUPFELD
Studio Edition Verticals

Model		Inches	Description	MSRP	SMP
P112		44	Polished Ebony	6,475	6,475
P118		46.5	Polished Ebony	6,740	6,712
P118		46.5	Polished White	6,880	6,831
P125		49	Polished Ebony	8,226	7,971

Europe Edition Verticals

Model		Inches	Description	MSRP	SMP
P116E		46	Polished Ebony	9,599	9,532
P116E		46	Satin Mahogany/Walnut	10,498	10,332
P116E		46	Satin Cherry	11,403	11,136
P116E		46	Polished Mahogany/Walnut	10,198	10,065
P116E		46	Polished Cherry/White	11,403	11,136
P122E		48	Polished Ebony	10,650	10,467
P122E		48	Satin Mahogany/Walnut	11,950	11,622
P122E		48	Satin Cherry	12,457	12,073
P122E		48	Polished Mahogany/Walnut	11,252	11,002
P122E		48	Polished Cherry	12,150	11,800
P122E		48	Polished Bubinga	13,330	12,849
P122E		48	Polished White	12,457	12,073
P132E		52	Polished Ebony	11,282	11,028
P132E		52	Satin Mahogany/Walnut	12,595	12,196
P132E		52	Satin Cherry	14,206	13,628
P132E		52	Polished Mahogany/Walnut	11,885	11,564
P132E		52	Polished Cherry/White	13,089	12,635
P132E		52	Polished Bubinga	15,740	14,991

Studio Edition Grands

Model	Feet	Inches	Description	MSRP	SMP
F 148	4	10	Polished Ebony	18,029	17,026
F 148	4	10	Polished Mahogany/Walnut	19,079	17,959
F 148	4	10	Polished White	18,279	17,248
F 160	5	3	Polished Ebony	20,829	19,515
F 160	5	3	Polished Mahogany/Walnut	21,689	20,279
F 160	5	3	Polished White	21,531	20,139
F 188	6	2	Polished Ebony	29,756	27,450
F 188	6	2	Polished Mahogany/Walnut	30,370	27,996
F 188	6	2	Polished White	30,458	28,074
F 213	7		Polished Ebony	34,409	31,586
F 213	7		Polished White	38,391	35,125

HUPFELD *(continued)*
Europe Edition Grands

Model	Feet	Inches	Description	MSRP	SMP
F 160E	5	3	Polished Ebony	32,919	30,261
F 160E	5	3	Polished Mahogany/Walnut	35,585	32,631
F 160E	5	3	Polished Cherry/Bubinga/White	38,345	35,084
F 175E	5	9	Polished Ebony	36,374	33,332
F 175E	5	9	Polished Mahogany/Walnut	45,838	41,745
F 175E	5	9	Polished Bubinga/White	48,598	44,198
F 190E	6	3	Polished Ebony	43,472	39,642
F 190E	6	3	Polished Mahogany/Walnut	45,838	41,745
F 190E	6	3	Polished Bubinga/White	48,598	44,198
F 210E	6	10.5	Polished Ebony	48,598	44,198
F 230E	7	6.5	Polished Ebony	56,484	51,208

IRMLER
Studio Edition Verticals

Model	Inches	Description	MSRP	SMP
P112	44	Polished Ebony	6,475	6,475
P118	46.5	Polished Ebony	6,740	6,712
P118	46.5	Polished White	6,880	6,831
P125	49	Polished Ebony	8,226	7,971

Art Design Verticals

Model	Inches	Description	MSRP	SMP
Da Vinci	47.5	Polished Ebony w/Verone Veneer Liner	9,531	9,077
Gina	48.5	Polished Ebony	10,514	9,910
Monique	49	Polished Ebony	11,480	10,729
Louis	49	Polished Ebony	11,127	10,430
Titus	49	Polished Ebony	11,480	10,729
Alexa	49	Polished Ebony	13,087	12,091
Carlo	49	Polished Ebony	13,414	12,368
Monet	49	Polished Ebony w/Verone Veneer Inner Fallboard & Lid	10,065	9,530
Van Gogh	50.5	Polished Ebony w/Vavone Front Liner Panels & Legs	12,738	11,795

Supreme Edition Verticals

Model	Inches	Description	MSRP	SMP
SP118	46.5	Polished Ebony	8,373	8,096
SP121	48	Polished Ebony	8,943	8,579
SP125	49	Polished Ebony	9,818	9,320
SP132	52	Polished Ebony	10,888	10,227

Professional Edition Verticals

Model	Inches	Description	MSRP	SMP
P116E	46	Polished Ebony	9,599	9,135
P116E	46	Satin Mahogany/Walnut	10,498	9,897
P116E	46	Satin Cherry	11,403	10,664
P116E	46	Polished Mahogany/Walnut	10,198	9,642
P116E	46	Polished Cherry/White	11,403	10,664
P122E	48	Polished Ebony	10,650	10,025
P122E	48	Satin Mahogany/Walnut	11,950	11,127

Model	Feet	Inches	Description	MSRP	SMP

IRMLER *(continued)*

Model	Feet	Inches	Description	MSRP	SMP
P122E		48	Satin Cherry	12,457	11,557
P122E		48	Polished Mahogany/Walnut	11,252	10,536
P122E		48	Polished Cherry	12,150	11,297
P122E		48	Polished Bubinga	13,330	12,297
P122E		48	Polished White	12,457	11,557
P132E		52	Polished Ebony	11,282	10,561
P132E		52	Satin Mahogany/Walnut	12,595	11,674
P132E		52	Satin Cherry	14,206	13,039
P132E		52	Polished Mahogany/Walnut	11,885	11,072
P132E		52	Polished Cherry/White	13,089	12,092
P132E		52	Polished Bubinga	15,740	14,339

Studio Edition Grands

Model	Feet	Inches	Description	MSRP	SMP
F148	4	10	Polished Ebony	18,029	16,279
F148	4	10	Polished Mahogany/Walnut	19,079	17,169
F148	4	10	Polished White	18,279	16,491
F160	5	3	Polished Ebony	20,829	18,652
F160	5	3	Polished Mahogany/Walnut	21,689	19,381
F160	5	3	Polished White	21,531	19,247
F188	6	2	Polished Ebony	29,756	26,217
F188	6	2	Polished Mahogany/Walnut	30,370	26,737
F188	6	2	Polished White	30,458	26,812
F213	7		Polished Ebony	36,409	31,855
F213	7		Polished White	38,391	33,535

Professional Edition Grands

Model	Feet	Inches	Description	MSRP	SMP
F160E	5	3	Polished Ebony	32,919	28,897
F160E	5	3	Polished Mahogany/Walnut	35,585	31,157
F160E	5	3	Polished Cherry	38,345	33,496
F160E	5	3	Polished White	38,345	33,496
F160E	5	3	Polished Bubinga	38,345	33,496
F175E	5	9	Polished Ebony	36,374	31,825
F175E	5	9	Polished Mahogany/Walnut	38,740	33,831
F175E	5	9	Polished White	41,500	36,169
F175E	5	9	Polished Bubinga	41,500	36,169
F190E	6	3	Polished Ebony	43,472	37,841
F190E	6	3	Polished Mahogany/Walnut	45,838	39,846
F190E	6	3	Polished White	48,598	42,185
F190E	6	3	Polished Bubinga	48,598	42,185
F210E	6	10.5	Polished Ebony	48,598	42,185
F230E	7	6.5	Polished Ebony	56,484	48,868

Model	Feet	Inches	Description	MSRP	SMP
KAWAI					
Verticals					
K-15		44	Continental Polished Ebony	5,595	5,595
K-15		44	Continental Polished Mahogany	5,895	5,895
K-15		44	Continental Polished Snow White	5,995	5,995
506N		44.5	Satin Ebony/Mahogany	5,595	5,595
508		44.5	Satin Mahogany	6,595	6,590
K-200		45	Satin and Polished Ebony	7,795	7,590
K-200		45	Satin and Polished Mahogany	8,495	8,190
K-200NKL		45	Satin and Polished Ebony with Nickel Trim	8,095	7,890
ST-1		46	Satin Ebony/Oak/Walnut/Cherry	8,495	8,190
ST-1		46	Polished Ebony	8,895	8,590
K-300		48	Satin and Polished Ebony	11,795	10,990
K-300		48	Satin and Polished Mahogany	12,495	11,590
K-300		48	Polished Snow White	12,695	11,790
K-300NKL		48	Satin and Polished Ebony with Nickel Trim	12,095	11,290
K-400		48	Polished Ebony	12,495	11,590
K-400NKL		48	Polished Ebony with Nickel Trim	12,795	11,890
K-500		51	Satin and Polished Ebony	15,295	13,990
K-500		51	Polished Sapele Mahogany	17,195	15,590
K-800		53	Polished Ebony	24,195	21,590
AnyTime (Silent) Verticals					
K-200 ATX3-CA		45	AnyTime Polished Ebony w/CA Sound	12,095	11,290
K-300 AURES		48	AnyTime Polished Ebony w/Soundboard Speaker	16,895	15,390
K-500 AURES		51	AnyTime Polished Ebony w/Soundboard Speaker	20,695	18,590
Grands					
GL-10	5		Satin and Polished Ebony	16,195	15,590
GL-10	5		Polished Ebony with Nickel Trim	17,095	16,390
GL-10	5		Polished Mahogany/Snow White	17,795	16,990
GL-10	5		French Provincial Polished Mahogany	19,095	18,190
GL-20	5	2	Satin and Polished Ebony	19,095	18,190
GL-20	5	2	Polished Mahogany	21,295	20,190
GL-20	5	2	Polished Snow White	21,295	20,190
GL-30	5	5	Satin and Polished Ebony	29,495	27,590
GL-30	5	5	Polished Sapele Mahogany	35,495	32,990
GL-30	5	5	Satin Dark Walnut	35,495	32,990
GL-30	5	5	Polished Snow White	33,995	31,590
GX-1 BLK	5	5	Satin and Polished Ebony	36,195	33,590
GX-1 BLK	5	5	Polished Dark Walnut	40,895	37,790
GL-40	5	11	Satin and Polished Ebony	34,895	32,390
GL-40	5	11	Polished Sapele Mahogany	41,095	37,990
GL-40	5	11	Satin Dark Walnut	41,095	37,990
GX-2 BLK	5	11	Satin and Polished Ebony	41,795	38,590
GX-2 BLK	5	11	Satin Walnut/Cherry/Oak	46,195	42,590
GX-2 BLK	5	11	Polished Walnut/Sapeli Mahogany	48,195	44,390

Model	Feet	Inches	Description	MSRP	SMP
KAWAI *(continued)*					
GX-2 BLK	5	11	Polished Snow White	44,395	40,990
GL-50	6	2	Polished Ebony	39,995	36,990
GX-3 BLK	6	2	Satin and Polished Ebony	53,495	49,190
GX-5 BLK	6	7	Satin and Polished Ebony	60,695	55,590
GX-6 BLK	7		Satin and Polished Ebony	67,995	62,190
GX-7 BLK	7	6	Satin and Polished Ebony	78,695	71,790
EX-L	9	1	Polished Ebony	180,695	180,695
AnyTime (Silent) Grands					
GL-30 ATX2-SS	5	5	AnyTime Polished Ebony w/Soundboard Speaker	34,695	32,190

KAWAI, SHIGERU

Grands

Model	Feet	Inches	Description	MSRP	SMP
SK-2	5	11	Polished Ebony	66,395	57,400
SK-2	5	11	Polished Sapele Mahogany	76,495	66,000
SK-3	6	2	Polished Ebony	77,595	67,000
SK-3	6	2	Polished Sapele Mahogany	89,195	76,800
SK-3	6	2	Polished Pyramid Mahogany	103,295	88,800
SK-5	6	7	Polished Ebony	89,395	77,000
SK-6	7		Polished Ebony	100,795	86,700
SK-7	7	6	Polished Ebony	111,795	96,000
SK-EX	9	1	Polished Ebony	197,595	197,595

KAYSERBURG

Verticals

Model	Feet	Inches	Description	MSRP	SMP
KA1		48	Polished Ebony	15,995	12,990
KA1		48	Polished Walnut	16,795	13,590
KA2		48.5	Polished Ebony	16,995	13,595
KA2		48.5	Polished Walnut	17,795	14,235
KA3		49.5	Polished Ebony	18,495	14,795
KA3		49.5	Polished Walnut	19,995	15,995
KA5		51	Polished Ebony	20,995	16,190
KA6		52	Polished Ebony	21,495	16,495

Grands

Model	Feet	Inches	Description	MSRP	SMP
KA151	5		Polished Ebony	38,995	31,195
KA160	5	3	Polished Ebony	47,995	38,395
KA180	5	9	Polished Ebony	59,995	52,990
KA212	7		Polished Ebony	76,000	67,087
KA243	8		Polished Ebony	86,000	75,783
KA275	9		Polished Ebony	147,500	129,261

Model	Feet	Inches	Description	MSRP	SMP
KINGSBURG					
Verticals					
LM 116		46	Chippendale Polished Walnut	6,610	5,893
KG 120		48	Polished Ebony	9,459	7,326
KU 120		48	Polished Ebony	8,815	6,114
KU 120		48	Satin and Polished Mahogany/Walnut	9,146	6,334
KG 122		48	Polished Ebony	10,085	7,657
KF 122		48	Polished Ebony	13,473	9,440
KF 123		50	Polished White & Red	13,480	9,862
KG 123		50	Decorator Satin Walnut	12,402	9,321
KU 123		50	Decorator Satin Walnut	9,917	6,996
KG 125		50	Polished Ebony	10,367	7,998
KU 125		50	Polished Ebony	9,917	6,775
KU 125		50	Polished Ebony w/Inlay	10,602	7,216
KU 125		50	Satin and Polished Mahogany/Walnut	10,469	6,996
KF 126		50	Satin Walnut	14,720	10,744
KF 128		50	Polished Ebony	14,498	11,626
KF 133		52	Polished Ebony	16,483	12,508
KG 133		52	Polished Ebony	12,497	9,421
KU 133		52	Polished Ebony	10,574	7,437
KU 133		52	Polished Mahogany/Walnut	11,003	7,657
Grands					
KF 158	5	3	Polished Ebony	25,909	25,859
KG 158	5	3	Polished Ebony	19,840	13,611
KG 158	5	3	Polished Ebony w/Inlay	20,942	14,272
KG 158	5	3	Polished Mahogany/Walnut	20,391	14,052
KG 175	5	9	Polished Ebony	22,320	14,006
KF 185	6	1	Polished Ebony	33,020	32,970
KG 185	6	1	Polished Ebony	24,250	15,375
KG 185	6	1	Polished Ebony w/Inlay	25,904	16,036
KG 185	6	1	Polished Mahogany/Walnut	25,352	15,816
KF 228	7	4	Polished Ebony	69,458	64,195
KNABE, WM.					
Baltimore Series Verticals					
WV 43		43	Continental Polished Ebony	7,519	5,663
WV 243F		43	French Provincial Satin Cherry	8,910	6,094
WV 243T		43	Satin Mahogany/Walnut	8,910	6,094
WV 115		45	Satin Ebony	9,797	6,607
WV 115		45	Polished Ebony	8,910	6,094
WV 115		45	Polished Mahogany/Walnut	10,024	6,710
WV 118H		46.5	Satin Ebony	10,360	6,936
WV 118H		46.5	Polished Ebony	10,024	6,710

Model	Feet	Inches	Description	MSRP	SMP

KNABE, WM. *(continued)*
Academy Series Verticals

Model	Feet	Inches	Description	MSRP	SMP
WMV 245		45	Satin Ebony	9,689	6,504
WMV 245		45	Polished Ebony	9,246	6,299
WMV 247		46.5	Satin Ebony/Walnut	11,138	7,348
WMV 247		46.5	Polished Ebony	10,803	7,143
WMV 647F		46.5	French Provincial Satin Cherry	10,803	7,143
WMV 647R		46.5	Renaissance Satin Walnut	10,803	7,143
WMV 647T		46.5	Satin Mahogany	10,803	7,143
WMV 121M		47.5	Satin Ebony	11,138	7,348
WMV 121M		47.5	Polished Ebony	10,803	7,143
WMV 132		52	Satin Ebony	13,702	8,826
WMV 132		52	Polished Ebony	13,031	8,416

Concert Artist Series Verticals

Model	Feet	Inches	Description	MSRP	SMP
WKV 118F		46.5	French Provincial Lacquer Semigloss Cherry	15,594	9,896
WKV 118R		46.5	Renaissance Lacquer Satin Ebony	15,594	9,896
WKV 118R		46.5	Renaissance Lacquer Semigloss Walnut	15,594	9,896
WKV 118T		46.5	Lacquer Semigloss Mahogany	15,594	9,896
WKV 121		48	Satin Ebony	16,265	10,327
WKV 121		48	Polished Ebony	15,594	9,896
WKV 132MD		52	Satin Ebony	17,822	11,169
WKV 132MD		52	Polished Ebony	16,265	10,327

Baltimore Series Grands

Model	Feet	Inches	Description	MSRP	SMP
WG 49	4	9	Satin Ebony	19,661	12,218
WG 49	4	9	Polished Ebony	18,179	11,374
WG 49	4	9	Polished Mahogany/Walnut	20,407	12,628
WG 54	5	4	Satin Ebony	22,278	13,698
WG 54	5	4	Polished Ebony	20,720	12,854
WG 54	5	4	Polished Mahogany/Walnut	22,613	13,924
WG 54	5	4	Polished Ebony w/Bubinga or Pommele Accents	25,955	15,814
WSG 54	5	4	M Leg w/Bubinga or Pommele Accents	29,632	17,929
WG 59	5	9	Satin Ebony	27,512	16,677
WG 59	5	9	Polished Ebony	25,620	15,607
WG 61	6	1	Satin Ebony	28,961	17,519
WG 61	6	1	Polished Ebony	27,512	16,677

Academy Series Grands

Model	Feet	Inches	Description	MSRP	SMP
WMG 610	5	9	Satin Ebony	30,854	18,567
WMG 610	5	9	Polished Ebony	29,297	17,724
WMG 660	6	1	Satin Ebony	34,531	20,684
WMG 660	6	1	Polished Ebony	33,082	19,840
WFM 700T	6	10	Satin Ebony	37,873	22,594
WFM 700T	6	10	Polished Ebony	36,424	21,752

Model	Feet	Inches	Description	MSRP	SMP

KNABE, WM. *(continued)*
Concert Artist Series Grands

Model	Feet	Inches	Description	MSRP	SMP
WKG 53	5	3	Satin Ebony	37,094	22,162
WKG 53	5	3	Polished Ebony	35,980	21,526
WKG 58	5	8	Satin Ebony	45,671	27,034
WKG 58	5	8	Polished Ebony	44,557	26,395
WKG 70	7		Satin Ebony	62,715	36,773
WKG 70	7		Polished Ebony	61,601	36,137
WKG 76	7	6	Satin Ebony	64,835	37,944
WKG 76	7	6	Polished Ebony	63,829	37,410
WKG 90	9	2	Satin Ebony	164,419	94,761
WKG 90	9	2	Polished Ebony	159,964	92,234

KRAUSE BERLIN, ERNST
Verticals

Model	Feet	Inches	Description	MSRP	SMP
KC-123		48.5	Polished Ebony	10,590	8,790
KC-123		48.5	Polished Mahogany/Walnut	11,590	9,690
KC-126		49.5	Polished Ebony	11,590	9,690
KC-126		49.5	Polished Mahogany/Walnut	12,590	10,490
KC-133		52.5	Polished Ebony	14,540	12,090

Grands

Model	Feet	Inches	Description	MSRP	SMP
KC-160	5	3	Polished Ebony	29,000	23,990
KC-160	5	3	Polished Mahogany/Walnut	33,200	27,590
KC-170	5	7	Polished Ebony	31,540	26,190
KC-170	5	7	Polished Mahogany/Walnut	34,550	28,690
KC-186	6	1	Polished Ebony	35,750	29,690
KC-186	6	1	Polished Mahogany/Walnut	38,750	32,190

MASON & HAMLIN
Verticals

Model	Feet	Inches	Description	MSRP	SMP
50		50	Satin Ebony	32,226	29,424
50		50	Polished Ebony	30,185	27,624
50		50	Cambridge Collection, Polished Ebony w/Bubinga or Macassar	35,287	30,324

Grands

Model	Feet	Inches	Description	MSRP	SMP
B	5	4	Satin Ebony	78,214	66,153
B	5	4	Polished Ebony	76,173	64,453
B	5	4	Polished Mahogany/Walnut	81,308	68,730
B	5	4	Polished Pyramid Mahogany	98,983	83,453
B	5	4	Polished Rosewood	90,275	76,200
B	5	4	Polished Bubinga	93,479	78,869

Model	Feet	Inches	Description	MSRP	SMP
MASON & HAMLIN *(continued)*					
B	5	4	Polished Macassar Ebony	98,983	83,453
A	5	8	Satin Ebony	79,438	67,173
A	5	8	Polished Ebony	77,398	65,473
A	5	8	Polished Mahogany/Walnut	82,531	69,750
A	5	8	Polished Pyramid Mahogany	100,208	84,473
A	5	8	Polished Rosewood	91,500	77,220
A	5	8	Polished Bubinga	94,703	79,889
A	5	8	Polished Macassar Ebony	100,208	84,473
AA	6	4	Satin Ebony	90,387	76,293
AA	6	4	Polished Ebony	88,346	74,593
AA	6	4	Polished Mahogany/Walnut	93,118	78,568
AA	6	4	Polished Pyramid Mahogany	106,995	90,128
AA	6	4	Polished Rosewood	98,265	82,855
AA	6	4	Polished Bubinga	101,462	85,517
AA	6	4	Polished Macassar Ebony	106,995	90,128
BB	7		Satin Ebony	102,293	86,211
BB	7		Polished Ebony	100,252	84,511
BB	7		Polished Mahogany/Walnut	103,800	87,465
BB	7		Polished Pyramid Mahogany	123,589	103,950
BB	7		Polished Rosewood	116,197	97,793
BB	7		Polished Bubinga	119,080	100,193
BB	7		Polished Macassar Ebony	123,589	103,950
CC	9	4	Satin Ebony	151,093	126,861
CC	9	4	Polished Ebony	149,053	125,161
CC	9	4	Polished Mahogany/Walnut	159,541	133,898
CC	9	4	Polished Pyramid Mahogany	181,635	152,303
CC	9	4	Polished Rosewood	168,612	141,454
CC	9	4	Polished Bubinga	174,263	146,161
CC	9	4	Polished Macassar Ebony	181,635	152,303
VX	9	4	Satin Ebony	181,706	152,361
VX	9	4	Polished Ebony	179,665	150,661
VX	9	4	Polished Mahogany/Walnut	190,153	159,398
VX	9	4	Polished Pyramid Mahogany	212,248	177,803
VX	9	4	Polished Rosewood	199,224	166,954
VX	9	4	Polished Bubinga	204,875	171,661
VX	9	4	Polished Macassar Ebony	212,248	177,803
Grands			Cambridge Collection, add	8,000	6,800
Artist Series Verticals					
MHA 123U		48	Polished Ebony	9,895	9,895
MHA 131U		51	Polished Ebony	11,834	11,834
Artist Series Grands					
MHA 160G	5	3	Polished Ebony	18,265	18,265
MHA 188G	6	2	Polished Ebony	23,346	23,346

Model	Feet	Inches	Description	MSRP	SMP

MASON & HAMLIN (continued)
Classic Series Verticals

Model	Feet	Inches	Description	MSRP	SMP
MHC 120U		47	Polished Ebony	7,540	7,540

Classic Series Grands

Model	Feet	Inches	Description	MSRP	SMP
MHC 150G	4	11	Polished Ebony	14,977	14,977
MHC 170G	5	6	Polished Ebony	15,908	15,908

PALATINO
Verticals

Model	Feet	Inches	Description	MSRP	SMP
PUP-22C		48	Polished Mahogany/Cherry	5,000	5,000
PUP-22C		48	Satin Walnut	5,000	5,000
PUP-123T		48	Torino Polished Ebony	5,900	5,900
PUP-123T		48	Torino Polished Dark Walnut	6,200	6,200
PUP-125		50	Satin and Polished Ebony	5,950	5,950
PUP-125		50	Polished Mahogany/White	5,950	5,950
PUP-126		50	Capri Polished Ebony	6,900	6,900
PUP-126		50	Capri Polished Dark Walnut	7,500	7,500

Grands

Model	Feet	Inches	Description	MSRP	SMP
PGD-50	5		Milano Polished Ebony	12,000	12,000
PGD-50	5		Milano Polished Dark Walnut	12,500	12,500
PGD-59	5	9	Roma Polished Ebony	13,400	13,400
PGD-62	6	2	Firenze Polished Ebony	15,400	15,400

PEARL RIVER
Verticals

Model	Feet	Inches	Description	MSRP	SMP
UP 109D		43	Continental Polished Ebony	4,895	4,700
UP 109D		43	Continental Polished Mahogany	5,095	4,900
EU 110		43	Polished Ebony	5,050	4,790
EU 110 Silent		43	Polished Ebony w/Silent System	8,295	7,190
EU 111PA		43	French Provincial Satin Cherry	6,195	5,590
EU 111PB		43	Mediterranean Satin Walnut	6,195	5,590
EU 111PC		43	Italian Provincial Satin Mahogany	6,195	5,590
UP 115E		45	Satin Ebony/Mahogany (School)	8,095	5,590
UP 115M5		45	Polished Ebony	5,195	4,990
UP 115M5		45	Polished Mahogany/Walnut/White	5,395	5,190
EU 118S		46.5	Polished Ebony w/Silver Hardware	5,695	5,390
EU 118S		46.5	Polished Mahogany/Walnut w/Silver Hardware	6,195	5,590
PE 121		48	Two-Tone Polished Ebony w/Sapele Mahogany Accents	7,595	6,990
EU 122		48	Polished Ebony	6,995	5,990
EU 122		48	Polished Mahogany/Walnut/White	7,095	6,190
EU 122		48	Satin Cherry	7,095	6,190
EU 122S		48	Polished Ebony w/Silver Hardware	7,095	6,190

Model	Feet	Inches	Description	MSRP	SMP

PEARL RIVER *(continued)*

Model	Feet	Inches	Description	MSRP	SMP
EU 122 Silent		48	Polished Ebony w/Silent System	9,395	8,390
EU 131		52	Polished Ebony	7,995	6,700

Grands

Model	Feet	Inches	Description	MSRP	SMP
GP 150	4	11	Hand-rubbed Satin Ebony	12,995	9,962
GP 150	4	11	Polished Ebony	12,395	9,548
GP 150	4	11	Polished Mahogany/Walnut/White	12,995	9,962
GP 150	4	11	Polished Sapele Mahogany/Artisan Walnut	13,695	10,445
GP 150SP	4	11	Polished Ebony w/Silver Plate/Hardware	12,995	9,962
GP 160	5	3	Hand-rubbed Satin Ebony	14,495	10,997
GP 160	5	3	Polished Ebony	13,995	10,652
GP 160SP	5	3	Polished Ebony w/Silver Plate/Hardware	14,495	10,997
GP 160	5	3	Polished Mahogany/Walnut/White	14,495	10,997
GP 160	5	3	Polished Sapele Mahogany/Artisan Walnut	15,195	11,479
GP 160 SP	5	3	Polished White w/Silver Plate/Hardware	15,495	11,686
GP 160SP	5	3	Polished Red w/Silver Plate/Hardware	16,495	12,376
GP 170	5	7	Hand-rubbed Satin Ebony	17,195	12,859
GP 170	5	7	Polished Ebony	16,495	12,376
GP 170	5	7	Polished Sapele Mahogany/Artisan Walnut	17,495	13,066
GP 188A	6	2	Polished Ebony	19,695	14,583

PERZINA

Verticals

Model	Feet	Inches	Description	MSRP	SMP
GP-112 Kompact		45	Continental Polished Ebony	8,890	8,000
GP-112 Kompact		45	Continental Polished Walnut/Mahogany	9,450	8,250
GP-112 Kompact		45	Continental Polished White	9,780	8,490
GP-115 Merit		45	Polished Ebony	9,660	8,430
GP-115 Merit		45	Polished Mahogany/Walnut	10,220	8,690
GP-115 Merit		45	Polished White	10,550	8,900
GP-115 Merit		45	Queen Anne Polished Ebony	10,220	8,600
GP-115 Merit		45	Queen Anne Polished Mahogany/Walnut	11,045	8,920
GP-115 Merit		45	Queen Anne Polished White	11,375	9,140
GP-122 Konsumat		48	Polished Ebony	10,990	9,090
GP-122 Konsumat		48	Polished Ebony with Chrome Hardware	12,090	10,000
GP-122 Konsumat		48	Polished Mahogany/Walnut	11,375	9,400
GP-122 Konsumat		48	Polished White	11,580	9,590
GP-122 Konsumat		48	Queen Anne Polished Ebony	11,375	9,380
GP-122 Konsumat		48	Queen Anne Polished Mahogany/Walnut	12,200	9,590
GP-122 Konsumat		48	Queen Anne Polished White	12,500	9,800
GP-122 Balmoral		48	Designer Polished Ebony	12,285	9,300
GP-122 Balmoral		48	Designer Polished Ebony/Bubinga (two-tone)	13,300	10,840
GP-129 Kapitol		51	Polished Ebony	12,240	10,220
GP-129 Kapitol		51	Polished Mahogany/Walnut	12,860	10,420

Model	Feet	Inches	Description	MSRP	SMP
PERZINA *(continued)*					
GP-129 Kapitol		51	Polished White	13,520	10,630
GP-129 Kapitol		51	Queen Anne Polished Ebony	13,520	10,420
GP-129 Kapitol		51	Queen Anne Polished Mahogany/Walnut	13,565	10,630
GP-129 Kapitol		51	Queen Anne Polished White	14,290	10,840
GP-130 Konzert		52	Polished Ebony	14,840	11,460
Grands					
GBT-152 Prysm	5	1	Polished Ebony	17,260	16,440
GBT-152 Prysm	5	1	Polished Mahogany/Walnut	18,530	17,650
GBT-152 Prysm	5	1	Polished White	18,750	17,860
GBT-152 Prysm	5	1	Designer Polished Mahogany/Walnut with Burled Walnut Inlay	20,490	19,520
GBT-152 Prysm	5	1	Designer Queen Anne or Empire Polished Ebony	17,590	16,760
GBT-152 Prysm	5	1	Designer Queen Anne or Empire Polished Mahogany/Walnut	18,880	17,980
GBT-152 Prysm	5	1	Designer Queen Anne or Empire Polished White	19,090	18,180
GBT-160 Sylvr	5	4	Polished Ebony	19,630	18,690
GBT-160 Sylvr	5	4	Polished Mahogany/Walnut	20,840	19,850
GBT-160 Sylvr	5	4	Polished White	21,030	20,020
GBT-160 Sylvr	5	4	Designer Polished Mahogany/Walnut with Burled Walnut Inlay	26,180	24,930
GBT-160 Sylvr	5	4	Designer Queen Anne or Empire Polished Ebony	19,970	19,020
GBT-160 Sylvr	5	4	Designer Queen Anne or Empire Polished Mahogany/Walnut	21,180	20,170
GBT-160 Sylvr	5	4	Designer Queen Anne or Empire Polished White	21,330	20,320
GBT-175 Granit	5	10	Polished Ebony	20,620	19,640
GBT-175 Granit	5	10	Polished Mahogany/Walnut	21,830	20,790
GBT-175 Granit	5	10	Polished White	22,030	20,980
GBT-175 Granit	5	10	Designer Polished Mahogany/Walnut with Burled Walnut Inlay	27,180	25,880
GBT-175 Granit	5	10	Designer Queen Anne or Empire Polished Ebony	20,960	19,960
GBT-175 Granit	5	10	Designer Queen Anne or Empire Polished Mahogany/Walnut	22,180	21,120
GBT-175 Granit	5	10	Designer Queen Anne or Empire Polished White	22,370	21,300
GBT-187 Royal	6	2	Polished Ebony	21,620	20,590
GBT-187 Royal	6	2	Polished Mahogany/Walnut	22,840	21,750
GBT-187 Royal	6	2	Polished White	23,030	21,930
GBT-187 Royal	6	2	Designer Polished Mahogany/Walnut with Burled Walnut Inlay	28,160	26,820
GBT-187 Royal	6	2	Designer Queen Anne or Empire Polished Ebony	21,950	20,910
GBT-187 Royal	6	2	Designer Queen Anne or Empire Polished Mahogany/Walnut	23,180	22,070
GBT-187 Royal	6	2	Designer Queen Anne or Empire Polished White	23,360	22,250

Model	Feet	Inches	Description	MSRP	SMP

PETROF
Most models are also available in finishes other than those shown here.

Verticals

Model	Feet	Inches	Description	MSRP	SMP
P 118 C1		46.25	Chippendale Polished Ebony		32,430
P 118 D1		46.25	Demi-Chippendale Polished Ebony		32,430
P 118 G2		46.25	Polished Ebony		25,690
P 118 M1		46.25	Polished Ebony		28,550
P 118 P1		46.25	Polished Ebony		28,550
P 118 R1		46.25	Rococo Satin White w/Gold Trim		34,248
P 118 S1		46.25	Continental Polished Ebony/White		25,090
P 122 N1		47.75	Polished Ebony		31,118
P 125 F1		49.25	Polished Ebony		32,012
P 125 G1		49.25	Polished Ebony		34,778
P 125 M1		49.25	Polished Ebony		33,498
P 127 NEXT		49.5	Satin Ebony with Chrome Legs		44,998
P 127 NEXT		49.5	Satin Wood Tones with Chrome Legs		46,000
P 131 M1		51	Polished Ebony		44,168
P 135 K1		53	Polished Ebony		52,564

Grands

Model	Feet	Inches	Description	MSRP	SMP
P 159	5	2	Bora Polished Ebony		87,058
P 159	5	2	Bora Demi-Chippendale Polished Ebony		95,020
P 173	5	6	Breeze Polished Ebony		91,748
P 173	5	6	Breeze Chippendale Polished Ebony		110,258
P 173	5	6	Breeze Demi-Chippendale Polished Ebony		108,068
P 173	5	6	Breeze Klasik Polished Ebony		100,666
P 173	5	6	Breeze Rococo Satin White w/Gold Trim		110,568
P 194	6	3	Storm Polished Ebony		96,310
P 194	6	3	Storm Styl Polished Ebony		104,812
P 210	6	10	Pasat Polished Ebony		137,640
P 237	7	9	Monsoon Polished Ebony		218,216
P 284	9	2	Mistral Polished Ebony		290,812
Grands			Mahogany/Walnut Upcharge		2,600
Grands			White or Color Upcharge		1,880

Petrof, Ant. Verticals

Model	Feet	Inches	Description	MSRP	SMP
136		53.5	Polished Ebony		38,632

Petrof, Ant. Grands

Model	Feet	Inches	Description	MSRP	SMP
225	7	4	Polished Ebony		187,278
275	9		Polished Ebony		252,328

PRAMBERGER

Legacy Series Verticals

Model	Feet	Inches	Description	MSRP	SMP
LV-110		43	Continental Polished Ebony	8,348	5,765
LV-43F		43	French Provincial Satin Cherry	9,019	6,197

Model	Feet	Inches	Description	MSRP	SMP
PRAMBERGER (*continued*)					
LV-43T		43	Satin Mahogany/Walnut	9,019	6,197
LV-115		45	Satin Ebony	9,797	6,607
LV-115		45	Polished Ebony	9,019	6,197
LV-115		45	Polished Mahogany/Walnut	10,024	6,710
LV-118		46.5	Satin Ebony	10,576	7,040
LV-118		46.5	Polished Ebony	9,797	6,607
Signature Series Verticals					
PV-118F/R/T		46.5	Decorator Satin Cherry/Mahogany/Walnut	11,138	7,348
PV-118S		46.5	Satin Ebony	11,474	7,574
PV-118S		46.5	Polished Ebony	10,803	7,143
PV-121		47.5	Satin Ebony	13,031	8,416
PV-121		47.5	Polished Ebony	12,252	7,984
PV-132		52	Satin Ebony	14,480	9,259
PV-132		52	Polished Ebony	13,702	8,826
J.P. Pramberger Platinum Series Verticals					
JP-132		52	Satin Ebony	18,157	11,374
JP-132		52	Polished Ebony	16,708	10,532
Legacy Series Grands					
LG-149	4	9	Satin Ebony	19,661	12,218
LG-149	4	9	Polished Ebony	18,179	11,374
LG-149	4	9	Polished Mahogany/Walnut	20,407	12,628
LG-157	5	2	Satin Ebony	22,278	13,698
LG-157	5	2	Polished Ebony	20,720	12,854
LG-157	5	2	Polished Ebony w/Bubinga or Pommele Accents	25,955	15,814
LG-157	5	2	Polished Fire Red	27,848	16,882
LG-175	5	9	Satin Ebony	27,404	16,677
LG-175	5	9	Polished Ebony	25,620	15,607
Signature Series Grands					
PS-157	5	2	Satin Ebony	27,512	16,677
PS-157	5	2	Polished Ebony	25,955	15,814
PS-157	5	2	Polished Ebony w/Bubinga or Pommele Accents	30,411	18,362
PS-175	5	9	Satin Ebony	29,740	17,929
PS-175	5	9	Polished Ebony	28,183	17,087
PS-185	6	1	Satin Ebony	30,854	18,567
PS-185	6	1	Polished Ebony	29,297	17,724
PS-208	6	10	Satin Ebony	41,150	23,232
PS-208	6	10	Polished Ebony	37,094	22,162
J.P. Pramberger Platinum Series Grands					
JP-179L	5	10	Satin Ebony	47,671	28,204
JP-179L	5	10	Polished Ebony	46,341	27,465
JP-179LF	5	10	French Provincial Satin Ebony	55,696	32,745
JP-179LF	5	10	French Provincial Lacquer Semigloss Cherry	55,696	32,745

Model	Feet	Inches	Description	MSRP	SMP

PRAMBERGER *(continued)*

Model	Feet	Inches	Description	MSRP	SMP
JP-208B	6	10	Satin Ebony	60,487	35,498
JP-208B	6	10	Polished Ebony	59,265	34,759
JP-228C	7	6	Satin Ebony	65,829	38,582
JP-228C	7	6	Polished Ebony	65,159	38,149
JP-280E	9	2	Polished Ebony	194,496	111,918

RITMÜLLER

Performance Verticals

Model	Feet	Inches	Description	MSRP	SMP
UP 110RB		43	French Provincial Satin Cherry	7,295	5,700
UP 110RB1		43	Italian Provincial Satin Walnut	7,295	5,700
UP 110R2		43	Polished Ebony	5,595	4,990
UP 110R2		43	Polished Mahogany	5,695	5,190
UP 120RE		47.25	Satin Mahogany	8,495	6,500
UP 121RB		47.6	Polished Ebony	7,395	6,190
UP 121RB		47.6	Polished Mahogany/Walnut/White	7,895	6,390

Premium Verticals

Model	Feet	Inches	Description	MSRP	SMP
UH 121R		48	Chippendale Polished Ebony	10,395	8,500
UH 121R		48	Chippendale Polished Sapele Mahogany	10,795	8,790
UH 121RA		48	Polished Ebony	10,295	8,390
UH 121RA Silent		48	Polished Ebony w/Silent System	13,795	10,790
UH 132R		52	Polished Ebony	12,595	9,790

Performance Grands

Model	Feet	Inches	Description	MSRP	SMP
R8	4	11	Polished Ebony	14,695	10,590
R8 SP	4	11	Polished Ebony w/Silver Plate/Hardware	15,595	11,190
R8	4	11	Polished Mahogany/White	15,595	11,190
R9	5	3	Polished Ebony	16,195	11,590
R9	5	3	Polished Mahogany/White	16,695	12,190
R9 SP	5	3	Polished White w/Silver Plate/Hardware	17,695	12,790

Premium Grands

Model	Feet	Inches	Description	MSRP	SMP
GH 148R	4	10	Polished Ebony	17,395	12,590
GH 148R	4	10	Polished Sapele Mahogany	17,995	13,590
GH 160R	5	3	Hand-rubbed Satin Ebony	20,995	15,790
GH 160R	5	3	Polished Ebony	20,195	14,790
GH 160R	5	3	Polished Sapele Mahogany	20,995	15,790
GH 170R	5	7	Polished Ebony	22,195	17,390
GH 188R	6	2	Polished Ebony	27,195	20,990
GH 212R	7		Polished Ebony	76,000	51,667
GH 243R	8		Polished Ebony	86,000	58,333
GH 275R	9		Polished Ebony	147,500	99,333

Model	Feet	Inches	Description	MSRP	SMP

RÖNISCH

Verticals

Model	Feet	Inches	Description	MSRP	SMP
118 K		46.5	Polished Ebony	22,428	22,428
118 K		46.5	Satin Mahogany/Walnut	23,604	23,604
118 K		46.5	Polished Mahogany/Walnut	27,720	27,720
118 K		46.5	Satin Cherry	24,024	24,024
118 K		46.5	Satin Beech/Alder/Ash/Oak	22,722	22,722
118 K		46.5	Polished White	24,570	24,570
118 K		46.5	Satin Swiss Pear/Indian Apple	24,654	24,654
118 KI		46.5	Polished Mahogany w/Vavona Inlays	28,770	28,770
118 KI		46.5	Polished Walnut w/Burled Walnut Inlays	28,980	28,980
118 KI		46.5	Polished Cherry w/Yew Inlays	29,400	29,400
125 K		49	Polished Ebony	24,780	24,780
125 K		49	Satin Mahogany/Walnut	25,830	25,830
125 K		49	Polished Mahogany/Walnut	30,198	30,198
125 K		49	Satin Cherry	25,746	25,746
125 K		49	Polished White	26,964	26,964
125 K		49	Satin Swiss Pear/Indian Apple	30,828	30,828
125 K		49	Carl Ronisch Edition Polished Burl Walnut	34,314	34,314
125 KI		49	Polished Mahogany w/Vavona Inlays	31,080	31,080
125 KI		49	Polished Walnut w/Burled Walnut Inlays	31,500	31,500
125 KI		49	Polished Cherry w/Yew Inlays	32,130	32,130
132 K		52	Polished Ebony	27,930	27,930
132 K		52	Satin Mahogany/Walnut	28,308	28,308
132 K		52	Polished Mahogany/Walnut	32,634	32,634
132 K		52	Polished White	30,114	30,114
132 K		52	Satin Swiss Pear/Indian Apple	33,936	33,936
132 K		52	Polished Bubinga	33,570	33,570
132 K		52	Carl Ronisch Edition Polished Burl Walnut	37,884	37,884
132 KI		52	Polished Mahogany w/Vavona Inlays	35,280	35,280
132 KI		52	Polished Walnut w/Burled Walnut Inlays	35,700	35,700
132 KI		52	Polished Cherry w/Yew Inlays	36,330	36,330

Grands

Model	Feet	Inches	Description	MSRP	SMP
175 K	5	9	Polished Ebony	68,894	68,894
175 K	5	9	Satin Mahogany/Walnut	70,452	70,452
175 K	5	9	Polished Mahogany/Walnut	81,438	81,438
175 K	5	9	Satin Cherry	73,568	73,568
175 K	5	9	Polished White	72,808	72,808
175 K	5	9	Polished Bubinga	85,728	85,728
175 K	5	9	Polished Rosewood	92,378	92,378
175 K	5	9	Carl Ronisch Edition Polished Burl Walnut	96,292	96,292
175 K	5	9	Carl Ronisch Edition Polished Vavona	96,292	96,292
175 K	5	9	Carl Ronisch Edition Polished Pyramid Mahogany	100,206	100,206
175 KI	5	9	Polished Mahogany w/Vavona Inlays	99,066	99,066
175 KI	5	9	Polished Walnut w/Burled Walnut Inlays	101,004	101,004

Model	Feet	Inches	Description	MSRP	SMP

RÖNISCH *(continued)*

Model	Feet	Inches	Description	MSRP	SMP
175 KI	5	9	Polished Cherry w/Yew Inlays	103,740	103,740
186 K	6	1	Polished Ebony	74,746	74,746
186 K	6	1	Satin Mahogany/Walnut	77,520	77,520
186 K	6	1	Polished Mahogany/Walnut	88,502	88,502
186 K	6	1	Satin Cherry	79,458	79,458
186 K	6	1	Polished White	78,660	78,660
186 K	6	1	Polished Bubinga	91,618	91,618
186 K	6	1	Polished Rosewood	98,268	98,268
186 K	6	1	Carl Ronisch Edition Polished Burl Walnut	102,182	102,182
186 K	6	1	Carl Ronisch Edition Polished Vavona	102,182	102,182
186 K	6	1	Carl Ronisch Edition Polished Pyramid Mahogany	106,096	106,096
186 KI	6	1	Polished Mahogany w/Vavona Inlays	104,956	104,956
186 KI	6	1	Polished Walnut w/Burled Walnut Inlays	107,274	107,274
186 KI	6	1	Polished Cherry w/Yew Inlays	110,390	110,390
210 K	6	10.5	Polished Ebony	86,156	86,156
210 K	6	10.5	Satin Mahogany/Walnut	89,080	89,080
210 K	6	10.5	Polished Mahogany/Walnut	98,600	98,600
210 K	6	10.5	Polished White	89,658	89,658
210 K	6	10.5	Polished Bubinga	108,800	108,800
210 K	6	10.5	Polished Rosewood	112,200	112,200
210 K	6	10.5	Carl Ronisch Edition Polished Burl Walnut	106,250	106,250
210 K	6	10.5	Carl Ronisch Edition Polished Vavona	106,250	106,250
210 K	6	10.5	Carl Ronisch Edition Polished Pyramid Mahogany	112,200	112,200
210 KI	6	10.5	Polished Mahogany w/Vavona Inlays	113,560	113,560
210 KI	6	10.5	Polished Walnut w/Burled Walnut Inlays	116,960	116,960
210 KI	6	10.5	Polished Cherry w/Yew Inlays	120,360	120,360

SAMICK

Verticals

Model		Inches	Description	MSRP	SMP
JS-43		43	Continental Satin Ebony	8,549	6,158
JS-43		43	Continental Polished Ebony	7,719	5,638
JS-143F		43	French Provincial Satin Cherry	8,549	6,158
JS-143T		43	Satin Mahogany	8,549	6,158
JS-115		45	Satin Ebony	9,269	6,358
JS-115		45	Polished Ebony	8,549	6,158
JS-115		45	Polished Mahogany/Walnut	9,059	6,458
JS-247		46.5	Institutional Satin Ebony	11,019	7,598
JS-247		46.5	Institutional Polished Ebony	10,299	7,178
JS-247		46.5	Institutional Satin Walnut	11,019	7,598
JS-118H		46.5	Satin Ebony	9,989	6,978
JS-118H		46.5	Polished Ebony	9,269	6,558
JS-121M		48	Satin Ebony	11,019	7,598
JS-121M		48	Polished Ebony	10,299	7,178

Model	Feet	Inches	Description	MSRP	SMP
SAMICK (continued)					
JS-132		52	Satin Ebony	13,389	8,939
JS-132		52	Polished Ebony	12,359	8,418
Grands					
SIG-49	4	9	Satin Ebony	18,179	11,918
SIG-49	4	9	Polished Ebony	16,809	11,098
SIG-54	5	4	Satin Ebony	21,629	13,978
SIG-54	5	4	Polished Ebony	19,569	12,638
SIG-54	5	4	Polished Fire-Engine Red	26,469	16,858
SIG-54	5	4	Polished Ebony w/Bubinga or Pommele Accents	24,509	15,738
SIG-57	5	7	Satin Ebony	25,029	16,038
SIG-57	5	7	Polished Ebony	23,479	15,118
SIG-57L	5	7	Empire Satin Ebony	27,809	17,698
SIG-57L	5	7	Empire Polished Ebony	26,469	16,858
SIG-61	6	1	Satin Ebony	27,089	17,278
SIG-61	6	1	Polished Ebony	25,439	16,258
SIG-61L	6	1	Empire Satin Ebony	29,659	18,818
SIG-61L	6	1	Empire Polished Ebony	28,119	17,898
NSG Series Grands					
NSG 158	5	2	Satin Ebony	25,495	19,198
NSG 158	5	2	Polished Ebony	23,995	18,198
NSG 175	5	7	Satin Ebony	27,995	20,998
NSG 175	5	7	Polished Ebony	26,495	19,998
NSG 186	6	1	Satin Ebony	30,795	22,998
NSG 186	6	1	Polished Ebony	29,395	21,998

SAUTER

Standard wood veneers are walnut, mahogany, ash, and alder.

Classic Line Verticals

Model	Feet	Inches	Description	MSRP	SMP
112		44	Carus Polished Ebony	21,900	21,900
112		44	Carus Satin Walnut	21,500	21,500
116		46	Cosmo Polished Ebony	24,500	24,500
116		46	Cosmo Satin Walnut	23,500	23,500
116		46	Vision Polished Ebony	27,900	27,900
116		46	Vision Satin Standard Wood	26,900	26,900
116		46	Vision Polished White	28,900	28,900
116		46	Nova Polished Ebony	28,900	28,900
116		46	Nova Satin Maple/Walnut	26,500	26,500
116		46	Nova Satin Peartree/Cherry	27,900	27,900
122		48	Schulpiano Satin Beech/Black Ash	33,000	33,000
122		48	Ragazza Polished Ebony	38,000	38,000
122		48	Ragazza Satin Cherry	37,500	37,500
122		48	Ragazza Polished Cherry/Yew	44,000	44,000
122		48	Vista Polished Ebony	41,000	41,000
122		48	Vista Satin Maple	39,000	39,000

Model	Feet	Inches	Description	MSRP	SMP
SAUTER *(continued)*					
122		48	Vista Satin Cherry	41,000	41,000
122		48	Master Class Polished Ebony	48,500	48,500
130		51	Master Class Polished Ebony	54,500	54,500
130		51	Competence Polished Ebony	46,500	46,500
130		51	Competence Satin Walnut	44,000	44,000
Designed by Peter Maly Verticals					
116		46	Concent Satin Ebony	32,000	32,000
116		46	Concent Polished Ebony	34,000	34,000
116		46	Accento Satin/Polished Ebony	35,000	35,000
116		46	Accento Satin Ebony/Polished White	35,000	35,000
116		46	Accento Classico Satin/Polished Ebony	36,500	36,500
116		46	Accento Classico Polished Ebony	37,000	37,000
122		48	Concent Satin Ebony	38,000	38,000
122		48	Concent Polished Ebony	39,000	39,000
122		48	Pure Basic Satin Ebony/Walnut	41,000	41,000
122		48	Pure Basic Satin White	41,000	41,000
122		48	Pure Basic Satin White/Maple	41,000	41,000
122		48	Pure Noble Polished Ebony/Veneers	50,000	50,000
122		48	Pure Noble Polished White/Red	52,000	52,000
122		48	Rondo Polished Ebony	45,000	45,000
122		48	Rondo Satin Wenge	41,000	41,000
122		48	Vitrea Colored Ebony with Glass	42,500	42,500
122		48	Rhapsody Satin Walnut/Polished Ebony	43,000	43,000
122		48	Peter Maly Artes Polished Ebony	53,000	53,000
122		48	Peter Maly Artes Polished Palisander/Macassar	54,000	54,000
122		48	Peter Maly Artes Polished White	54,000	54,000
Classic Line Grands					
60	5	3	Alpha Polished Ebony	100,000	100,000
160	5	3	Alpha Satin Standard Wood Veneers	94,000	94,000
160	5	3	Chippendale Satin Cherry	104,000	104,000
160	5	3	Chippendale Satin Standard Wood Veneers	100,000	100,000
160	5	3	Noblesse Satin Cherry	111,000	111,000
160	5	3	Noblesse Polished Cherry	119,000	119,000
160	5	3	Noblesse Satin Burl Walnut	114,000	114,000
160	5	3	Noblesse Satin Standard Wood Veneers	109,000	109,000
160	5	3	Noblesse Polished Standard Wood Veneers	117,000	117,000
185	6	1	Delta Polished Ebony	113,000	113,000
185	6	1	Delta Polished Ebony w/Burl Walnut	117,000	117,000
185	6	1	Delta Polished Pyramid Mahogany	124,000	124,000
185	6	1	Delta Polished Bubinga	123,000	123,000
185	6	1	Delta Polished Rio Palisander	123,000	123,000
185	6	1	Delta Satin Maple with Silver	105,000	105,000
185	6	1	Delta Polished White	113,000	113,000
185	6	1	Delta Satin Standard Wood Veneers	103,000	103,000
185	6	1	Chippendale Satin Cherry	115,000	115,000

Model	Feet	Inches	Description	MSRP	SMP
SAUTER *(continued)*					
185	6	1	Chippendale Satin Standard Wood Veneers	111,000	111,000
185	6	1	Noblesse Satin Cherry	122,000	122,000
185	6	1	Noblesse Polished Cherry	136,000	136,000
185	6	1	Noblesse Satin Burl Walnut	128,000	128,000
185	6	1	Noblesse Satin Standard Wood Veneers	118,000	118,000
185	6	1	Noblesse Polished Standard Wood Veneers	133,000	133,000
220	7	3	Omega Polished Ebony	143,000	143,000
220	7	3	Omega Polished Burl Walnut	157,000	157,000
220	7	3	Omega Polished Pyramid Mahogany	157,000	157,000
220	7	3	Omega Satin Standard Wood Veneers	134,000	134,000
275	9		Concert Polished Ebony	246,000	246,000
Designed by Peter Maly Grands					
210	6	11	Vivace Polished Ebony	159,000	159,000
210	6	11	Vivace Satin Wood Veneers	149,000	149,000
210	6	11	Vivace Polished White	158,000	158,000
230	7	7	Ambiente Polished Ebony	180,000	180,000
230	7	7	Ambiente Polished Ebony w/Crystals	206,000	206,000

SCHIMMEL

Classic Series Verticals

Model		Inches	Description	MSRP	SMP
C 116		46	Tradition Polished Ebony	24,915	20,932
C 116		46	Tradition Polished Mahogany/White	28,083	23,466
C 116		46	Tradition Satin Walnut/Cherry/Alder	24,915	20,932
C 116		46	Modern Polished Ebony	28,875	24,100
C 116		46	Modern Polished White	32,043	26,634
C 116		46	Modern Cubus Polished Ebony	28,875	24,100
C 116		46	Modern Cubus Polished White	32,043	26,634
C 120		48	Tradition Polished Ebony	27,028	22,622
C 120		48	Tradition Polished Mahogany/White	30,195	25,156
C 120		48	Tradition Satin Walnut/Cherry/Alder	27,028	22,622
C 120		48	Tradition Marketerie Polished Mahogany w/Inlay	32,305	26,844
C 120		48	Elegance Manhattan Polished Ebony	26,105	21,884
C 120		48	Elegance Manhattan Polished Mahogany/White	29,273	24,418
C 120		48	Royal Polished Ebony	29,665	24,732
C 120		48	Royal Intarsie Flora Polished Mahogany w/Inlays	34,945	28,956
C 121		48	Tradition Polished Ebony	27,705	23,164
C 121		48	Tradition Polished Mahogany/White	30,950	25,760
C 121		48	Tradition Satin Walnut/Cherry/Alder	27,705	23,164
C 121		48	Tradition Marketerie Polished Mahogany w/Inlay	33,245	27,596
C 121		48	Tradition Noblesse Polished Ebony w/Exotic-Wood Inlay Panels	30,950	25,760
C 121		48	Tradition Prestige Polished Ebony w/Exotic-Wood Inlay Panels	36,212	29,969
C 121		48	Elegance Manhattan Polished Ebony	26,758	22,406

Model	Feet	Inches	Description	MSRP	SMP
SCHIMMEL *(continued)*					
C 121		48	Elegance Manhattan Super Matte Satin Ebony w/Chrome Hardware	27,948	23,358
C 121		48	Royal Polished Ebony	30,475	25,380
C 121		48	Royal Intarsie Flora Polished Mahogany w/Inlays	36,015	29,812
C 123		48	Tradition Polished Ebony (limited edition)	29,863	24,890
C 126		50	Tradition Polished Ebony	32,833	27,266
C 126		50	Tradition Polished Mahogany	36,000	29,800
C 130		51	Tradition Polished Ebony	35,473	29,378
C 130		51	Tradition Polished Mahogany	38,640	31,912
Konzert Series Verticals					
K 122		48	Elegance Polished Ebony	36,398	30,118
K 125		49	Tradition Polished Ebony	39,038	32,230
K 125		49	Tradition Polished Mahogany	43,260	35,608
K 132		52	Tradition Polished Ebony	44,580	36,664
K 132		52	Tradition Polished Mahogany	48,803	40,042
Fridolin Schimmel Verticals					
F 116		46	Polished Ebony	7,838	7,270
F 116		46	Polished White	8,213	7,570
F 121		48	Polished Ebony	8,963	8,170
F 121		48	Polished Walnut/White	9,338	8,470
F 123		49	Polished Ebony	10,088	9,070
F 123		49	Polished Mahogany/White	10,463	9,370
Wilhelm Schimmel Verticals					
W 114		46	Tradition Polished Ebony	17,130	14,704
W 114		46	Tradition Polished Mahogany/White	19,770	16,816
W 114		46	Modern Polished Ebony	18,050	15,440
W 114		46	Modern Polished White	20,075	17,060
W 118		48	Tradition Polished Ebony	18,715	15,972
W 118		48	Tradition Polished Mahogany/White	21,353	18,082
W 123		49	Tradition Polished Ebony	20,298	17,238
W 123		49	Tradition Polished Mahogany/White	22,938	19,350
W 123		49	Tradition Polished Ebony	20,298	17,238
W 123		49	Tradition Polished Mahogany/White	22,938	19,350
Classic Series Grands					
C 169	5	7	Tradition Polished Ebony	67,938	55,350
C 169	5	7	Tradition Polished Mahogany/White	74,535	60,628
C 189	6	3	Tradition Polished Ebony	71,895	58,516
C 189	6	3	Tradition Polished Mahogany/White	78,495	63,796
C 213	7		Tradition Polished Ebony	78,495	63,796
C 213	7		Tradition Polished Mahogany/White	85,093	69,074
Konzert Series Grands					
K 175	5	9	Tradition Polished Ebony	86,870	70,496
K 175	5	9	Tradition Polished Mahogany/White	94,558	76,646

Model	Feet	Inches	Description	MSRP	SMP

SCHIMMEL (continued)

Model	Feet	Inches	Description	MSRP	SMP
K 195	6	5	Tradition Polished Ebony	94,558	76,646
K 195	6	5	Tradition Polished Mahogany/White	102,245	82,796
K 213	7		Glas Clear Acrylic and White or Black and Gold	320,313	257,250
K 213	7		Otmar Alt Polished Ebony w/Color Motifs	230,625	185,500
K 219	7	2	Tradition Polished Ebony	102,245	82,796
K 219	7	2	Tradition Polished Mahogany/White	109,933	88,946
K 230	7	6	Tradition Polished Ebony	117,620	95,096
K 256	8	4	Tradition Polished Ebony	132,995	107,396
K 280	9	2	Tradition Polished Ebony	153,495	123,796

Wilhelm Schimmel Grands

Model	Feet	Inches	Description	MSRP	SMP
W 180	6		Tradition Polished Ebony	41,413	34,130
W 180	6		Tradition Polished Mahogany/White	46,693	38,354
W 206	6	10	Tradition Polished Ebony	50,650	41,520
W 206	6	10	Tradition Polished Mahogany/White	55,930	45,744

SCHULZ, GEBR.
Verticals

Model	Feet	Inches	Description	MSRP	SMP
G-20		48	Polished Ebony	9,995	9,590
G-20		48	Hand-rubbed Satin Walnut	12,895	12,500

Grands

Model	Feet	Inches	Description	MSRP	SMP
G-58	5	5	Polished Ebony	18,995	18,995
G-86	6		Polished Ebony	23,995	23,995
G-288	9		Polished Ebony	49,995	49,995

SCHULZE POLLMANN
Studio Series Verticals

Model	Feet	Inches	Description	MSRP	SMP
SU118A		46	Polished Peacock Ebony	15,995	9,490
SU118A		46	Polished Peacock Mahogany/Walnut	16,995	10,090
SU122A		48	Polished Peacock Ebony	18,995	10,890
SU122A		48	Polished Peacock Mahogany/Walnut	19,995	11,490
SU122A		48	Polished Feather Mahogany	20,995	12,090
SU132A		52	Polished Peacock Ebony	23,995	13,490

Academy Series Verticals

Model	Feet	Inches	Description	MSRP	SMP
A-125E		50	Polished Ebony	26,995	14,890
A-125E		50	Polished Peacock Ebony	27,995	15,490
A-125E		50	Polished Peacock Mahogany	30,995	17,490
A-125E		50	Polished Peacock Walnut	31,995	18,090
A-125E		50	Polished Feather Mahogany	33,995	18,090

Studio Series Grands

Model	Feet	Inches	Description	MSRP	SMP
S148	4	10	Polished Ebony	18,995	18,490
SU148	4	10	Polished Peacock Ebony/Feather Mahogany	19,995	19,490

Model	Feet	Inches	Description	MSRP	SMP
SCHULZE POLLMANN (continued)					
S160	5	3	Polished Ebony	21,995	20,090
SU160	5	3	Polished Peacock Ebony/Feather Mahogany	22,995	21,090
S172A	5	8	Polished Ebony	24,995	22,490
SU172A	5	8	Polished Peacock Ebony/Feather Mahogany	25,995	23,490
S187A	6	2	Polished Ebony	27,995	25,490
SU187A	6	2	Polished Peacock Ebony/Feather Mahogany	28,995	27,490
Masterpiece Series Grands					
160/GK	5	3	Polished Ebony (spade leg)	55,995	55,995
160/GK	5	3	Polished Briar Mahogany (spade leg)	59,995	59,995
160/GK	5	3	Polished Feather Mahogany (spade leg)	63,995	63,995
197/G5	6	6	Polished Ebony (spade leg)	77,995	76,990
197/G5	6	6	Polished Briar Mahogany (spade leg)	80,995	80,995
197/G5	6	6	Polished Feather Mahogany (spade leg)	84,995	84,995

SCHUMANN
Verticals
Model	Feet	Inches	Description	MSRP	SMP
C1-112		44	Polished Ebony	5,995	4,990
C1-112		44	Polished Mahogany	6,195	5,390
K1-122		48	Polished Ebony	6,495	5,590
K1-122		48	Polished Mahogany	6,695	5,990
K1-122		48	Polished Walnut/White	6,695	6,190

Grands
Model	Feet	Inches	Description	MSRP	SMP
GP-152	5		Polished Ebony	11,900	9,590
GP-152	5		Polished Mahogany/White	12,900	10,390
GP-168	5	6	Polished Ebony	14,900	11,990
GP-168	5	6	Polished White	15,900	12,590
GP-186	6	2	Polished Ebony	18,995	13,190

SEILER
Seiler Verticals
Model	Feet	Inches	Description	MSRP	SMP
SE-112		43	Modern, Satin Ebony	36,189	27,778
SE-116		45	Primus, Polished Ebony	29,769	23,038
SE-116		45	Mondial, Polished Ebony	31,409	24,278
SE-116		45	Mondial, Polished Rosewood	42,539	32,518
SE-116		45	Konsole, Polished Ebony	34,595	26,598
SE-116		45	Konzept6, Satin White	41,759	31,898
SE-116		45	Impuls, Polished Ebony	37,579	28,818
SE-116		45	Impuls, Satin Wenge	38,979	29,838
SE-116		45	Clou, Polished Ebony	36,979	28,398
SE-116		45	Accent, Polished Ebony	36,979	28,398
SE-122		48	Primus, Polished Ebony	39,759	30,458
SE-126		49	Konsole, Polished Ebony	43,979	33,558

Model	Feet	Inches	Description	MSRP	SMP

SEILER (continued)

Model	Feet	Inches	Description	MSRP	SMP
SE-126		49	Konsole, Satin Walnut	45,319	34,578
SE-126		49	Attraction, Polished Ebony	47,069	35,818
SE-126		49	Attraction, Polished Ebony w/Ziricote	61,249	46,318
SE-132		52	Consert, Polished Ebony	53,969	40,978
SE-132		52	Consert, Polished Ebony w/SMR	56,749	43,038
SE-132		52	Consert, Polished Ebony w/Rec Panel	56,749	43,038
SE-132		52	Consert, Polished Ebony w/Rec Panel/SMR	59,529	45,098

Eduard Seiler ED Series Verticals

Model	Feet	Inches	Description	MSRP	SMP
ED-126		49	Primus, Satin Ebony	13,499	10,998
ED-126		49	Primus, Polished Ebony	12,960	10,598
ED-126M		49	Primus, Satin Ebony w/SMR	14,850	11,998
ED-126M		49	Primus, Polished Ebony w/SMR	14,299	11,598
ED-132		52	Konzert, Satin Ebony	14,299	11,598
ED-132		52	Konzert, Polished Ebony	13,790	11,198
ED-132M		52	Konzert, Satin Ebony w/SMR	15,930	12,798
ED-132M		52	Konzert, Polished Ebony w/SMR	15,199	12,198

Eduard Seiler ES Studio Series Verticals

Model	Feet	Inches	Description	MSRP	SMP
ES-126		49	Primus, Satin Ebony	28,995	22,990
ES-126		49	Primus, Polished Ebony	27,495	21,990
ES-132		52	Konzert, Satin Ebony	32,095	24,990
ES-132		52	Konzert, Polished Ebony	30,595	24,190

Johannes Seiler Verticals

Model	Feet	Inches	Description	MSRP	SMP
GS-110NDR		43	Continental Polished Ebony	9,639	9,198
GS-110NDR		43	Continental Polished Lacquer Dark Walnut	10,099	9,598
GS-110NDR		43	Continental Polished Fire-Engine Red	10,099	9,598
GS-110BDR		43	170th Anniv. Polished Grey w/Black Hardware	10,099	9,598
GS-110BDR		43	170th Anniv. Polished White w/Black Hardware	10,099	9,598
GS-112NDR		44	Polished Ebony	10,099	9,598
GS-112NDR		44	Polished Lacquer Dark Walnut	10,590	9,998
GS-112NDR		44	Polished Fire-Engine Red	10,590	9,998
GS-112BDR		44	170th Anniv. Polished White/Grey w/Black Hardware	10,590	9,998
GS-116N		45.5	Satin Ebony w/Nickel Hardware	9,779	8,640
GS-116N		45.5	Polished Ebony w/Nickel Hardware	9,679	8,240
GS-247		46.5	Satin Ebony	10,509	9,240
GS-247		46.5	Polished Ebony	9,779	8,640
GS-247		46.5	Satin Walnut	10,509	9,240
GS-118		47	Satin Ebony	9,989	8,840
GS-118		47	Polished Ebony	9,289	8,440
GS-121		47.5	Ditto, Polished Ebony w/Silver accent	11,949	9,840
GS-122		48.5	Satin Ebony	10,995	9,440
GS-122		48.5	Polished Ebony	9,989	8,840
GS-122N		48.5	Impulz, Polished Ebony	10,290	9,198
GS-122LID		48.5	Satin Dark Walnut	11,250	9,640

Model	Feet	Inches	Description	MSRP	SMP

SEILER *(continued)*

Seiler Grands

Model	Feet	Inches	Description	MSRP	SMP
SE-168	5	6	Virtuoso, Polished Ebony	99,289	74,538
SE-168	5	6	Virtuoso, Polished Mahogany	119,269	89,378
SE-186	6	2	Maestro, Polished Ebony	116,599	87,318
SE-186	6	2	Maestro, Polished Mahogany	124,939	93,498
SE-186	6	2	Maestro, Polished Rosewood	133,489	99,878
SE-186	6	2	Maestro, Matte Ebony Ceramic	139,189	103,998
SE-186	6	2	Maestro, Polished Ebony w/Ziricote	126,279	94,538
SE-186	6	2	Louvre, Polished Cherry	157,489	117,598
SE-186	6	2	Florenz, Polished Mahogany	157,489	117,598
SE-208	6	10	Professional, Polished Ebony	130,709	97,818
SE-242	8		Konzert, Polished Ebony	172,939	129,138
SE-278	9	2	Konzert, Polished Ebony	280,879	209,058

Eduard Seiler ED Series Grands

Model	Feet	Inches	Description	MSRP	SMP
ED-168	5	6	Virtuoso, Satin Ebony	37,720	28,940
ED-168	5	6	Virtuoso, Polished Ebony	37,180	28,540
ED-168HS	5	6	Heritage, Satin Ebony	46,999	35,798
ED-168HS	5	6	Heritage, Polished Ebony	45,759	34,998
ED-186	6	2	Maestro, Satin Ebony	45,890	34,800
ED-186	6	2	Maestro, Polished Ebony	44,550	34,000
ED-208	6	10	Conservatory Artist, Satin Ebony	63,179	47,798
ED-208	6	10	Conservatory Artist, Polished Ebony	58,320	44,198

Eduard Seiler ES Studio Series Grands

Model	Feet	Inches	Description	MSRP	SMP
ES-168	5	6	Virtuoso, Satin Ebony	61,079	46,598
ES-168	5	6	Virtuoso, Polished Ebony	59,579	45,198
ES-186	6	2	Maestro, Satin Ebony	66,599	52,598
ES-186	6	2	Maestro, Polished Ebony	65,099	51,198

Johannes Seiler Grands

Model	Feet	Inches	Description	MSRP	SMP
GS-150	5		Satin Ebony	18,549	14,418
GS-150	5		Polished Ebony	17,919	13,358
GS-150	5		Polished White/Fire-Engine Red	20,389	15,418
GS-150	5		Polished Ebony w/Bubinga Accents	20,389	15,418
GS-150	5		Polished Lacquer Dark Walnut	19,649	14,998
GS-150B	5		170th Anniv. Polished Grey w/Black Hardware	20,389	15,418
GS-150LN	5		Satin Ebony w/Nickel Hardware, round leg	21,629	16,458
GS-150LN	5		Polished Ebony w/Nickel Hardware, round leg	20,389	15,418
GS-150LN	5		Polished Ebony w/Bubinga Accents & Nickel Hardware, round leg	22,119	16,858
GS-160	5	3	Satin Ebony	25,395	19,798
GS-160	5	3	Polished Ebony	23,995	18,798
GS-160LN	5	3	Satin Ebony, round leg	28,595	22,198
GS-160LN	5	3	Polished Ebony, round leg	27,295	21,198
GS-175	5	9	Satin Ebony	27,795	21,598
GS-175	5	9	Polished Ebony	26,395	20,598

Model	Feet	Inches	Description	MSRP	SMP

SEILER *(continued)*

Model	Feet	Inches	Description	MSRP	SMP
GS-186	6	2	Satin Ebony	29,695	22,998
GS-186	6	2	Polished Ebony	28,595	22,198
GS-208	6	10	Satin Ebony	32,649	26,038
GS-208	6	10	Polished Ebony	31,499	24,998

STEINBERG, G.
Verticals

Model		Inches	Description	MSRP	SMP
RH-111 Nicosia		45	Polished Ebony	7,580	7,220
RH-111 Nicosia		45	Polished Mahogany/Walnut	7,800	7,430
RH-111 Nicosia		45	Polished White	8,020	7,640
RH-115 Slate		45	Polished Ebony	7,800	7,430
RH-115 Slate		45	Polished Mahogany/Walnut	7,930	7,550
RH-115 Slate		45	Polished White	8,170	7,780
RH-115 Slate		45	Queen Anne Polished Ebony	7,930	7,550
RH-115 Slate		45	Queen Anne Polished Mahogany/Walnut	8,040	7,660
RH-115 Slate		45	Queen Anne Polished White	8,280	7,880
RH-119 Splendit		47	Polished Ebony	8,250	7,860
RH-119 Splendit		47	Polished Mahogany/Walnut	8,480	8,070
RH-119 Splendit		47	Polished White	8,690	8,280
RH-119 Splendit		47	Queen Anne Polished Ebony	8,370	7,970
RH-119 Splendit		47	Queen Anne Polished Mahogany/Walnut	8,590	8,180
RH-119 Splendit		47	Queen Anne Polished White	8,790	8,380
RH-123 Performance		49	Polished Ebony	8,480	8,070
RH-123 Performance		49	Queen Anne Polished Ebony	8,690	8,280
RH-126 Sienna		50	Polished Ebony	9,130	8,700
RH-126 Sienna		50	Queen Anne Polished Ebony	9,340	8,900

Grands

Model	Feet	Inches	Description	MSRP	SMP
GBT-152 Sovereign	5	1	Polished Ebony	15,450	14,710
GBT-152 Sovereign	5	1	Polished Mahogany/Walnut	16,610	15,820
GBT-152 Sovereign	5	1	Polished White	16,970	16,160
GBT-152 Sovereign	5	1	Queen Anne or Empire Polished Ebony	15,880	15,120
GBT-152 Sovereign	5	1	Queen Anne or Empire Polished Mahogany/Walnut	17,110	16,290
GBT-152 Sovereign	5	1	Queen Anne or Empire Polished White	17,390	16,560
GBT-160 Stockholm	5	5	Polished Ebony	17,750	16,910
GBT-160 Stockholm	5	5	Polished Mahogany/Walnut	18,850	17,950
GBT-160 Stockholm	5	5	Polished White	19,070	18,160
GBT-160 Stockholm	5	5	Queen Anne or Empire Polished Ebony	18,050	17,190
GBT-160 Stockholm	5	5	Queen Anne or Empire Polished Mahogany/Walnut	19,370	18,450
GBT-160 Stockholm	5	5	Queen Anne or Empire Polished White	19,590	18,660
GBT-175 Schwerin	5	10	Polished Ebony	18,490	17,620
GBT-175 Schwerin	5	10	Polished Mahogany/Walnut	20,040	19,080
GBT-175 Schwerin	5	10	Polished White	20,250	19,280
GBT-175 Schwerin	5	10	Queen Anne or Empire Polished Ebony	19,070	18,160

Model	Feet	Inches	Description	MSRP	SMP

STEINBERG, G. *(continued)*

Model	Feet	Inches	Description	MSRP	SMP
GBT-175 Schwerin	5	10	Queen Anne or Empire Polished Mahogany/Walnut	20,380	19,410
GBT-175 Schwerin	5	10	Queen Anne or Empire Polished White	20,590	19,620
GBT-187 Amsterdam	6	2	Polished Ebony	19,730	18,790
GBT-187 Amsterdam	6	2	Polished Mahogany/Walnut	20,820	19,820
GBT-187 Amsterdam	6	2	Polished White	21,030	20,030
GBT-187 Amsterdam	6	2	Queen Anne or Empire Polished Ebony	20,060	19,100
GBT-187 Amsterdam	6	2	Queen Anne or Empire Polished Mahogany/Walnut	21,260	20,240
GBT-187 Amsterdam	6	2	Queen Anne or Empire Polished White	21,470	20,450

STEINBERG, WILH.

Performance Series Verticals

Model	Feet	Inches	Description	MSRP	SMP
P118		45.5	Polished Ebony	8,820	6,880
P118		45.5	Polished White	9,960	7,640
P118C		45.5	Polished Ebony w/Chrome Hardware	8,985	6,990
P118C		45.5	Polished White w/Chrome Hardware	10,125	7,750
P121		47.5	Polished Ebony	10,065	7,710
P121		47.5	Polished White	11,205	8,470
P125E		49.5	Polished Ebony	12,030	9,020
P125EC		49.5	Polished Ebony w/Chrome Hardware	12,195	9,130

Signature Series Verticals

Model	Feet	Inches	Description	MSRP	SMP
S125		49	Polished Ebony	34,155	23,770
S125		49	Polished White	36,990	25,660
S125		49	Satin Mahogany/Walnut	37,305	25,870
S125		49	Polished Alder	38,415	26,610
S130		51	Polished Ebony	40,365	27,910
S130		51	Polished White	43,500	30,000
S130		51	Satin Mahogany/Walnut	43,815	30,210
S130		51	Polished Alder	45,225	31,150

Performance Series Grands

Model	Feet	Inches	Description	MSRP	SMP
P152	5		Polished Ebony	22,450	15,967
P152	5		Polished White	23,940	16,960
P165	5	5	Polished Ebony	25,850	18,233
P165	5	5	Polished White	27,800	19,533
P178	5	10	Polished Ebony	35,530	24,687

Signature Series Grands

Model	Feet	Inches	Description	MSRP	SMP
S188	6	2	Polished Ebony	83,370	56,580
S212	6	11	Polished Ebony	92,670	62,780

Model	Feet	Inches	Description	MSRP	SMP
STEINGRAEBER & SÖHNE					

Prices include bench.

Verticals

Model	Feet	Inches	Description	MSRP	SMP
122 T		48	Satin and Polished Ebony	51,310	50,060
122 T		48	Satin and Polished White	52,280	51,030
122 T		48	Polished Ebony w/Twist & Change Panels	57,840	56,590
122 T		48	Satin Ordinary Veneers	62,550	61,300
122 T		48	Polished Ordinary Veneers	68,700	67,450
122 T		48	Satin Special Veneers	64,650	63,400
122 T		48	Polished Special Veneers	70,860	69,610
122 T		48	Satin Extraordinary Veneers	78,490	77,240
122 T		48	Polished Extraordinary Veneers	84,660	83,410
122 T-SFM		48	Satin and Polished Ebony	54,210	52,960
122 T-SFM		48	Satin and Polished White	55,200	53,950
122 T-SFM		48	Polished Ebony w/Twist & Change Panels	60,740	59,490
122 T-SFM		48	Satin Ordinary Veneers	65,440	64,190
122 T-SFM		48	Polished Ordinary Veneers	71,620	70,370
122 T-SFM		48	Satin Special Veneers	67,540	66,290
122 T-SFM		48	Polished Special Veneers	73,760	72,510
122 T-SFM		48	Satin Extraordinary Veneers	81,380	80,130
122 T-SFM		48	Polished Extraordinary Veneers	87,580	86,330
130 T-PS		51	Satin and Polished Ebony	65,320	64,070
130 T-PS		51	Satin and Polished White	66,310	65,060
130 T-PS		51	Polished Ebony w/Twist & Change Panels	71,850	70,600
130 T-PS		51	Satin Ordinary Veneers	76,550	75,300
130 T-PS		51	Polished Ordinary Veneers	82,710	81,460
130 T-PS		51	Satin Special Veneers	78,650	77,400
130 T-PS		51	Polished Special Veneers	84,870	83,620
130 T-PS		51	Satin Extraordinary Veneers	92,490	91,240
130 T-PS		51	Polished Extraordinary Veneers	98,690	97,440
130 T-SFM		51	Satin and Polished Ebony	66,600	65,350
130 T-SFM		51	Satin and Polished White	67,590	66,340
130 T-SFM		51	Polished Ebony w/Twist & Change Panels	73,130	71,880
130 T-SFM		51	Satin Ordinary Veneers	77,830	76,580
130 T-SFM		51	Polished Ordinary Veneers	84,010	82,760
130 T-SFM		51	Satin Special Veneers	79,930	78,680
130 T-SFM		51	Polished Special Veneers	86,110	84,860
130 T-SFM		51	Satin Extraordinary Veneers	93,770	92,520
130 T-SFM		51	Polished Extraordinary Veneers	99,930	98,680
138 K		54	Satin and Polished Ebony	69,270	68,020
138 K		54	Satin and Polished White	70,250	69,000
138 K		54	Polished Ebony w/Twist & Change Panels	75,780	74,530
138 K		54	Satin Ordinary Veneers	80,520	79,270
138 K		54	Polished Ordinary Veneers	86,680	85,430
138 K		54	Satin Special Veneers	82,620	81,370
138 K		54	Polished Special Veneers	88,800	87,550

Model	Feet	Inches	Description	MSRP	SMP
STEINGRAEBER & SÖHNE *(continued)*					
138 K		54	Satin Extraordinary Veneers	96,460	95,210
138 K		54	Polished Extraordinary Veneers	102,610	101,360
138 K-SFM		54	Satin and Polished Ebony	72,190	70,940
138 K-SFM		54	Satin and Polished White	73,170	71,920
138 K-SFM		54	Polished Ebony w/Twist & Change Panels	78,700	77,450
138 K-SFM		54	Satin Ordinary Veneers	83,420	82,170
138 K-SFM		54	Polished Ordinary Veneers	89,590	88,340
138 K-SFM		54	Satin Special Veneers	85,540	84,290
138 K-SFM		54	Polished Special Veneers	91,740	90,490
138 K-SFM		54	Satin Extraordinary Veneers	99,360	98,110
138 K-SFM		54	Polished Extraordinary Veneers	105,550	104,300
Grands					
A-170	5	7	Satin and Polished Ebony	120,390	119,140
A-170	5	7	Satin and Polished Ebony w/Mozart Rail	129,890	128,640
A-170	5	7	Satin and Polished White	123,060	121,810
A-170	5	7	Satin and Polished Ordinary Veneers	136,860	135,610
A-170	5	7	Satin and Polished Special Veneers	138,680	137,430
A-170	5	7	Satin and Polished Extraordinary Veneers	148,280	147,030
A-170 S	5	7	Studio Lacquer Anti-Scratch	116,420	115,170
B-192	6	3	Satin and Polished Ebony	138,620	137,370
B-192	6	3	Satin and Polished Ebony w/Mozart Rail	148,110	146,860
B-192	6	3	Satin and Polished White	141,290	140,040
B-192	6	3	Satin and Polished Ordinary Veneers	156,870	155,620
B-192	6	3	Satin and Polished Special Veneers	158,870	157,620
B-192	6	3	Satin and Polished Extraordinary Veneers	169,620	168,370
B-192 S	6	3	Studio Lacquer Anti-Scratch	134,110	132,860
C-212	7		Satin and Polished Ebony	158,050	156,800
C-212	7		Satin and Polished Ebony w/Sordino Pedal and Mozart Rail	179,190	177,940
C-212	7		Satin and Polished White	160,670	159,420
C-212	7		Satin and Polished Ordinary Veneers	177,530	176,280
C-212	7		Satin and Polished Special Veneers	179,760	178,510
C-212	7		Satin and Polished Extraordinary Veneers	191,650	190,400
C-212 S	7		Studio Lacquer Anti-Scratch	152,540	151,290
D-232	7	7	Satin and Polished Ebony	185,360	184,110
D-232	7	7	Satin and Polished Ebony w/Sordino Pedal and Mozart Rail	206,510	205,260
D-232	7	7	Satin and Polished White	187,920	186,670
D-232	7	7	Satin and Polished Ordinary Veneers	206,230	204,980
D-232	7	7	Satin and Polished Special Veneers	208,590	207,340
D-232	7	7	Satin and Polished Extraordinary Veneers	221,190	219,940
D-232 S	7	7	Studio Lacquer Anti-Scratch	179,650	178,400
E-272	8	11	Satin and Polished Ebony w/Sordino Pedal and Mozart Rail	274,130	272,880
E-272	8	11	Satin and Polished White w/Sordino Pedal and Mozart Rail	276,810	275,560

Model	Feet	Inches	Description	MSRP	SMP

STEINGRAEBER & SÖHNE (continued)

Model	Feet	Inches	Description	MSRP	SMP
E-272	8	11	Satin and Polished Ordinary Veneers w/Sordino Pedal and Mozart Rail	299,870	298,620
E-272	8	11	Satin and Polished Special Veneers w/Sordino Pedal and Mozart Rail	301,890	300,640
E-272	8	11	Satin and Polished Extraordinary Veneers w/Sordino Pedal and Mozart Rail	318,670	317,420

STEINWAY & SONS

These are the prices at the Steinway retail store in New York City, often used as a benchmark for Steinway prices throughout the country. Model K-52 in ebony and grand models in ebony, mahogany, and walnut include adjustable artist benches. Other models include regular wood bench. Wood-veneered models are in a semigloss finish called "satin lustre."

Verticals

Model	Feet	Inches	Description	MSRP	SMP
K-52		52	Satin Ebony	42,000	42,000
K-52		52	Polished Ebony	48,000	48,000
K-52		52	Mahogany	47,300	47,300
K-52		52	Walnut	49,000	49,000

Grands

Model	Feet	Inches	Description	MSRP	SMP
S	5	1	Satin and Polished Ebony	75,500	75,500
S	5	1	Polished Ebony w/Sterling Hardware	77,500	77,500
S	5	1	Polished White	86,100	86,100
S	5	1	Polished Custom Color	94,800	94,800
S	5	1	Mahogany	92,300	92,300
S	5	1	Walnut	93,400	93,400
S	5	1	Amberwood	98,600	98,600
S	5	1	Applewood	98,600	98,600
S	5	1	Dark Cherry	98,600	98,600
S	5	1	Figured Sapele	98,600	98,600
S	5	1	Figured Sycamore	98,600	98,600
S	5	1	Kewazinga Bubinga	98,600	98,600
S	5	1	Padauk	110,200	110,200
S	5	1	Santos Rosewood	110,200	110,200
S	5	1	East Indian Rosewood	114,400	114,400
S	5	1	Koa	114,400	114,400
S	5	1	African Pommele	115,400	115,400
S	5	1	Macassar Ebony	125,900	125,900
S	5	1	Ziricote	131,000	131,000
M	5	7	Satin and Polished Ebony	81,300	81,300
M	5	7	Polished Ebony w/Sterling Hardware	83,300	83,300
M	5	7	Polished White	91,900	91,900
M	5	7	Polished Custom Color	101,100	101,100
M	5	7	Polished Ebony w/White/Color Pops Accessories	97,300	97,300
M	5	7	Mahogany	98,300	98,300
M	5	7	Walnut	99,400	99,400
M	5	7	Amberwood	104,700	104,700
M	5	7	Applewood	104,700	104,700

Model	Feet	Inches	Description	MSRP	SMP
STEINWAY & SONS *(continued)*					
M	5	7	Dark Cherry	104,700	104,700
M	5	7	Figured Sapele	104,700	104,700
M	5	7	Figured Sycamore	104,700	104,700
M	5	7	Kewazinga Bubinga	104,700	104,700
M	5	7	Padauk	116,300	116,300
M	5	7	Santos Rosewood	116,300	116,300
M	5	7	Onyx Duet Polished Ebony	119,400	119,400
M	5	7	East Indian Rosewood	120,700	120,700
M	5	7	Koa	120,700	120,700
M	5	7	African Pommele	121,700	121,700
M	5	7	John Lennon Imagine Polished White	125,700	125,700
M	5	7	Macassar Ebony	132,300	132,300
M	5	7	Ziricote	137,400	137,400
M 1014A	5	7	Chippendale Mahogany	113,100	113,100
M 1014A	5	7	Chippendale Walnut	114,200	114,200
M 501A	5	7	Louis XV Walnut	145,700	145,700
M 501A	5	7	Louis XV East Indian Rosewood	166,700	166,700
M Sketch 1111	5	7	The Teague Satin and Polished Ebony (Spirio only, included)	125,300	125,300
M Sketch 1111	5	7	The Teague Walnut (Spirio only, included)	135,600	135,600
M			Spirio Play (playback only) Player Piano System, add	25,000	25,000
M			Spirio l r (playback & record) Player Piano System, add	40,000	40,000
O	5	10.5	Satin and Polished Ebony	90,300	90,300
O	5	10.5	Polished Ebony w/Sterling Hardware	92,300	92,300
O	5	10.5	Polished White	100,800	100,800
O	5	10.5	Polished Custom Color	110,900	110,900
O	5	10.5	Polished Ebony w/White/Color Pops Accessories	106,000	106,000
O	5	10.5	Mahogany	107,100	107,100
O	5	10.5	Walnut	108,100	108,100
O	5	10.5	Amberwood	113,300	113,300
O	5	10.5	Applewood	113,300	113,300
O	5	10.5	Dark Cherry	113,300	113,300
O	5	10.5	Figured Sapele	113,300	113,300
O	5	10.5	Figured Sycamore	113,300	113,300
O	5	10.5	Kewazinga Bubinga	113,300	113,300
O	5	10.5	Padauk	124,900	124,900
O	5	10.5	Santos Rosewood	124,900	124,900
O	5	10.5	Onyx Duet Polished Ebony	129,100	129,100
O	5	10.5	East Indian Rosewood	129,100	129,100
O	5	10.5	Koa	129,100	129,100
O	5	10.5	African Pommele	130,100	130,100
O	5	10.5	John Lennon Imagine Polished White	135,400	135,400
O	5	10.5	Macassar Ebony	140,600	140,600
O	5	10.5	Ziricote	145,700	145,700
A	6	2	Satin and Polished Ebony	104,200	104,200
A	6	2	Polished Ebony w/Sterling Hardware	106,200	106,200

Model	Feet	Inches	Description	MSRP	SMP
STEINWAY & SONS *(continued)*					
A	6	2	Polished White	116,900	116,900
A	6	2	Polished Custom Color	128,600	128,600
A	6	2	Polished Ebony w/White/Color Pops Accessories	122,100	122,100
A	6	2	Mahogany	124,200	124,200
A	6	2	Walnut	125,200	125,200
A	6	2	Amberwood	131,600	131,600
A	6	2	Applewood	131,600	131,600
A	6	2	Dark Cherry	130,400	130,400
A	6	2	Figured Sapele	129,400	129,400
A	6	2	Figured Sycamore	131,600	131,600
A	6	2	Kewazinga Bubinga	131,600	131,600
A	6	2	Padauk	145,200	145,200
A	6	2	Santos Rosewood	145,200	145,200
A	6	2	Onyx Duet Polished Ebony	143,100	143,100
A	6	2	East Indian Rosewood	149,400	149,400
A	6	2	Koa	149,400	149,400
A	6	2	African Pommele	153,600	153,600
A	6	2	John Lennon Imagine Polished White	158,900	158,900
A	6	2	Macassar Ebony	163,100	163,100
A	6	2	Ziricote	169,000	169,000
B	6	10.5	Satin and Polished Ebony	117,800	117,800
B	6	10.5	Polished Ebony w/Sterling Hardware	121,800	121,800
B	6	10.5	Polished White	131,400	131,400
B	6	10.5	Polished Custom Color	144,600	144,600
B	6	10.5	Polished Ebony w/White/Color Pops Accessories	135,600	135,600
B	6	10.5	Mahogany	137,800	137,800
B	6	10.5	Walnut	138,800	138,800
B	6	10.5	Amberwood	145,100	145,100
B	6	10.5	Applewood	145,100	145,100
B	6	10.5	Dark Cherry	144,000	144,000
B	6	10.5	Figured Sapele	143,000	143,000
B	6	10.5	Figured Sycamore	145,100	145,100
B	6	10.5	Kewazinga Bubinga	145,100	145,100
B	6	10.5	Padauk	158,800	158,800
B	6	10.5	Santos Rosewood	158,800	158,800
B	6	10.5	Onyx Duet Polished Ebony	156,600	156,600
B	6	10.5	East Indian Rosewood	162,900	162,900
B	6	10.5	Koa	162,900	162,900
B	6	10.5	African Pommele	167,100	167,100
B	6	10.5	John Lennon Imagine Polished White	172,400	172,400
B	6	10.5	Macassar Ebony	176,600	176,600
B	6	10.5	Ziricote	182,500	182,500
B	6	10.5	Astor Polished Ebony	127,800	127,800
B	6	10.5	Lenny Kravitz Macassar Ebony (Spirio l r only, included)	500,000	500,000
B	6	10.5	Black Diamond Ebony (Spirio l r only, included)	275,000	275,000
B	6	10.5	Black Diamond Macassar Ebony (Spirio l r only, included)	375,000	375,000

Model	Feet	Inches	Description	MSRP	SMP

STEINWAY & SONS *(continued)*

Model	Feet	Inches	Description	MSRP	SMP
B			Spirio Play (playback only) Player Piano System, add	25,000	25,000
B			Spirio I r (playback & record) Player Piano System, add	40,000	40,000
D	8	11.75	Satin and Polished Ebony	187,100	187,100
D	8	11.75	Polished Ebony w/Sterling Hardware	191,100	191,100
D	8	11.75	Polished White	206,300	206,300
D	8	11.75	Polished Custom Color	227,000	227,000
D	8	11.75	Polished Ebony w/White/Color Pops Accessories	208,300	208,300
D	8	11.75	Mahogany	218,900	218,900
D	8	11.75	Walnut	220,100	220,100
D	8	11.75	Amberwood	230,700	230,700
D	8	11.75	Applewood	230,700	230,700
D	8	11.75	Dark Cherry	227,500	227,500
D	8	11.75	Figured Sapele	224,300	224,300
D	8	11.75	Figured Sycamore	230,700	230,700
D	8	11.75	Kewazinga Bubinga	230,700	230,700
D	8	11.75	Padauk	247,600	247,600
D	8	11.75	Santos Rosewood	247,600	247,600
D	8	11.75	East Indian Rosewood	262,500	262,500
D	8	11.75	Koa	262,500	262,500
D	8	11.75	African Pommele	274,100	274,100
D	8	11.75	John Lennon Imagine Polished White	242,300	242,300
D	8	11.75	Macassar Ebony	283,700	283,700
D	8	11.75	Ziricote	293,400	293,400
D	8	11.75	Black Diamond Macassar Ebony (Spirio I r only, included)	585,000	585,000
D	8	11.75	Spirio I r (playback & record) Player Piano System, add	40,000	40,000
All Grands			Skyline, add'l	11,500	11,500

Steinway (Hamburg) Grands

I frequently get requests for prices of pianos made in Steinway's branch factory in Hamburg, Germany. Officially, these pianos are not sold in North America, but it is possible to order one through an American Steinway dealer, or to go to Europe and purchase one there. The following list shows approximately how much it would cost to purchase a Hamburg Steinway in Europe and have it shipped to the United States. The list was derived by taking the published retail price in Europe, subtracting the value-added tax not applicable to foreign purchasers, converting to U.S. dollars (the rate used here is 1 Euro = $1.20, but is obviously subject to change), and adding approximate charges for duty, air freight, crating, insurance, brokerage fees, and delivery. Only prices for grands in polished ebony are shown here. Caution: This list is published for general informational purposes only. The price that Steinway would charge for a piano ordered through an American Steinway dealer may be different. (Also, the cost of a trip to Europe to purchase the piano is not included.)

Model	Feet	Inches	Description	MSRP	SMP
S-155	5	1	Polished Ebony	94,700	94,700
M-170	5	7	Polished Ebony	97,900	97,900
O-180	5	10.5	Polished Ebony	107,400	107,400
A-188	6	2	Polished Ebony	110,100	110,100
B-211	6	11	Polished Ebony	126,900	126,900
C-227	7	5.5	Polished Ebony	143,300	143,300
D-274	8	11.75	Polished Ebony	191,800	191,800

Model	Feet	Inches	Description	MSRP	SMP

STORY & CLARK

All Story & Clark pianos include PNOscan, and USB and MIDI connectivity. In addition, all grands now include a QRS PNOmation player-piano system. Prices shown are those for online sales through www.qrsmusic.com.

Heritage Series Verticals

Model	Feet	Inches	Description	MSRP	SMP
H7		46	Academy Polished Ebony		5,395

Heritage Series Grands

Model	Feet	Inches	Description	MSRP	SMP
H50A	4	11	Prelude Polished Ebony/Mahogany		16,695
H60 QA	5		French Provincial Polished Ebony		17,495
H60 QA	5		French Provincial Satin Lacquer and Polished Mahogany		17,595
H60A	5	3	Academy Satin and Polished Ebony		17,495
H60A	5	3	Academy Polished Mahogany		17,495
H60A	5	3	Academy Polished White		17,995
H80	6	1	Professional Polished Ebony		21,395
H90	6	10	Semi-Concert Polished Ebony		28,795

WALTER, CHARLES R.

Verticals

Model	Feet	Inches	Description	MSRP	SMP
1520		43	Satin and Polished Walnut		20,150
1520		43	Satin and Polished Cherry		20,088
1520		43	Satin and Polished Oak		19,442
1520		43	Satin and Polished Mahogany		20,502
1520		43	Italian Provincial Satin and Polished Walnut		20,388
1520		43	Italian Provincial Satin and Polished Mahogany		20,542
1520		43	Italian Provincial Satin and Polished Oak		19,884
1520		43	Country Classic Satin and Polished Cherry		19,914
1520		43	Country Classic Satin and Polished Oak		19,576
1520		43	French Provincial Satin and Polished Oak		20,188
1520		43	French Provincial Satin and Polished Cherry/Walnut/Mahogany		20,776
1520		43	Riviera Satin and Polished Oak		19,588
1520		43	Queen Anne Satin and Polished Oak		20,348
1520		43	Queen Anne Satin and Polished Mahogany/Cherry		20,776
1500		45	Satin Ebony		18,778
1500		45	Semi-Gloss Ebony		19,130
1500		45	Polished Ebony (Lacquer)		19,342
1500		45	Polished Ebony (Polyester)		19,736
1500		45	Satin and Polished Oak		18,390
1500		45	Satin and Polished Walnut		18,976
1500		45	Satin and Polished Mahogany		19,248
1500		45	Satin and Polished Gothic Oak		18,996
1500		45	Satin and Polished Cherry		19,388
Verticals			Renner (German) action, add		1,500

Model	Feet	Inches	Description	MSRP	SMP

WALTER, CHARLES R. *(continued)*
Grands

Model	Feet	Inches	Description	MSRP	SMP
W-175	5	9	Satin Ebony		82,758
W-175	5	9	Semi-Polished Ebony		84,622
W-175	5	9	Polished Ebony (Lacquer)		86,622
W-175	5	9	Polished Ebony (Polyester)		88,622
W-175	5	9	Satin Mahogany/Walnut/Cherry		89,400
W-175	5	9	Semi-Polished Mahogany/Walnut/Cherry		90,600
W-175	5	9	Polished Mahogany/Walnut/Cherry		91,000
W-175	5	9	Open-Pore Walnut		87,400
W-175	5	9	Satin Oak		79,940
W-175	5	9	Chippendale Satin Mahogany/Cherry		93,400
W-175	5	9	Chippendale Semi-Polished Mahogany/Cherry		93,800
W-175	5	9	Chippendale Polished Mahogany/Cherry		94,200
W-190	6	4	Satin Ebony		87,000
W-190	6	4	Semi-Polished Ebony		88,000
W-190	6	4	Polished Ebony (Lacquer)		90,000
W-190	6	4	Polished Ebony (Polyester)		92,000
W-190	6	4	Satin Mahogany/Walnut/Cherry		92,800
W-190	6	4	Semi-Polished Mahogany/Walnut/Cherry		94,000
W-190	6	4	Polished Mahogany/Walnut/Cherry		94,400
W-190	6	4	Open-Pore Walnut		90,800
W-190	6	4	Satin Oak		84,940
W-190	6	4	Chippendale Satin Mahogany/Cherry		97,400
W-190	6	4	Chippendale Semi-Polished Mahogany/Cherry		97,800
W-190	6	4	Chippendale Polished Mahogany/Cherry		98,200

WEBER
Weber Verticals

Model	Feet	Inches	Description	MSRP	SMP
W114		45	Polished Ebony	6,390	6,080
W114		45	Polished Mahogany	6,690	6,280
W121		48	Polished Ebony	7,190	6,780
W121		48	Polished Mahogany/Walnut/White	7,490	6,980
W131		52	Polished Ebony	7,890	7,180

Albert Weber Verticals

Model	Feet	Inches	Description	MSRP	SMP
AW 121		48	Polished Ebony	11,890	9,980
AW 121		48	Satin Mahogany	11,990	10,380
AW 121E		48	Polished Ebony w/Chrome	12,790	10,980
AW 131		52	Satin Ebony	14,200	12,780
AW 131		52	Polished Ebony	14,090	11,980

Model	Feet	Inches	Description	MSRP	SMP

WEBER *(continued)*
Weber Grands

Model	Feet	Inches	Description	MSRP	SMP
W150	4	11	Polished Ebony	14,490	12,580
W150	4	11	Polished Mahogany/Walnut/White	14,790	12,980
W150SP	4	11	Polished Ebony w/Chrome	15,190	13,180
W150SP	4	11	Polished White w/Chrome	15,290	13,380
W157	5	2	Polished Ebony	15,490	13,380
W157	5	2	Polished Mahogany	15,990	13,980
W175	5	9	Polished Ebony	17,490	14,780
W185	6	1	Polished Ebony	21,490	17,780

Albert Weber Grands

Model	Feet	Inches	Description	MSRP	SMP
AW 185	6	1	Polished Ebony	37,550	30,180
AW 208	6	10	Polished Ebony	46,350	36,780
AW 228	7	6	Polished Ebony	64,390	50,780
AW 275	9		Polished Ebony	116,190	88,780

WERTHEIM
Verticals

Model	Feet	Inches	Description	MSRP	SMP
W121L		48	Polished Ebony	6,499	5,999
W123		48.5	Polished Ebony	6,999	6,499
W123		48.5	Polished Mahogany	7,299	6,999
WE123		48.5	Polished Ebony	8,999	8,499
WF125V1		49	Polished Ebony	17,999	16,999
WF125V3		49	Polished Ebony	11,999	11,299
W126		49.5	Polished Ebony	7,299	6,999

Grands

Model	Feet	Inches	Description	MSRP	SMP
W160	5	3	Polished Ebony	12,499	10,999
W160	5	3	Polished Mahogany	13,499	11,999
WF165	5	5	Polished Ebony	29,999	24,999
WE170	5	7	Polished Ebony	18,999	15,999
WE170	5	7	Polished Mahogany	19,999	14,999
WE186	6	1	Polished Ebony	22,999	19,999

Model	Feet	Inches	Description	MSRP	SMP

YAMAHA
Including Disklavier, Silent, and TransAcoustic Pianos

Verticals

Model	Feet	Inches	Description	MSRP	SMP
b1		43	Continental Polished Ebony	4,799	4,799
b1		43	Continental Polished Ebony with Chrome Accents	4,999	4,999
b1		43	Continental Polished White	4,999	4,999
M560		44	Hancock Satin Brown Cherry	7,899	7,899
b2		45	Polished Ebony	6,749	6,598
b2		45	Polished Ebony with Chrome Accents	6,949	6,798
b2		45	Polished Mahogany/Walnut/White	7,159	6,998
P22D		45	Satin Ebony	7,849	7,598
P22D		45	Satin Walnut/Dark Oak	8,199	7,998
P660		45	Sheraton Satin Brown Mahogany	9,979	9,979
P660		45	Queen Anne Satin Brown Cherry	9,979	9,979
b3		48	Polished Ebony	8,259	7,798
b3		48	Polished Ebony with Chrome Accents	8,459	7,998
b3		48	Polished Mahogany/Walnut/White	9,129	8,298
U1		48	Satin and Polished Ebony	11,399	11,399
U1		48	Satin American Walnut	13,499	13,499
U1		48	Polished Mahogany/White	13,499	13,499
YUS1		48	Satin and Polished Ebony	15,599	14,998
YUS1		48	Satin American Walnut	18,799	17,930
YUS1		48	Polished Mahogany/White	18,799	17,930
U3		52	Polished Ebony	14,559	14,098
U3		52	Satin American Walnut	16,599	16,398
U3		52	Polished Mahogany	16,599	16,398
YUS3		52	Polished Ebony	18,899	17,998
YUS3		52	Polished Mahogany	21,799	20,598
YUS5		52	Polished Ebony	20,999	19,978
SU7		52	Polished Ebony	39,999	38,390

Disklavier Verticals

Model	Feet	Inches	Description	MSRP	SMP
DU1ENST		48	Satin and Polished Ebony	29,099	27,558
DU1ENST		48	Satin American Walnut	31,199	29,698
DU1ENST		48	Polished Mahogany/White	31,199	29,698
DYUS1ENST		48	Satin and Polished Ebony	33,299	30,698
DYUS1ENST		48	Satin American Walnut	36,499	33,630
DYUS1ENST		48	Polished Mahogany/White	36,499	33,630
DYUS5ENST		52	Polished Ebony	38,699	35,678

Silent and TransAcoustic Verticals

Model	Feet	Inches	Description	MSRP	SMP
b1SC2		43	Polished Ebony	9,299	9,398
b1SC2		43	Polished Ebony with Chrome Accents	9,499	9,698
b1SC2		43	Polished White	9,499	9,698
b2SC2		45	Polished Ebony	11,249	10,298
b2SC2		45	Polished Ebony with Chrome Accents	11,449	10,498

Model	Feet	Inches	Description	MSRP	SMP
YAMAHA *(continued)*					
b2SC2		45	Polished Mahogany/Walnut/White	11,659	10,698
P22DSC2		45	Satin Ebony	12,349	11,298
P22DSC2		45	Satin Walnut/Dark Oak	12,699	11,698
b3SC2		48	Polished Ebony	12,759	11,498
b3SC2		48	Polished Ebony with Chrome Accents	12,959	11,698
b3SC2		48	Polished Mahogany/Walnut/White	13,629	11,998
U1SH2		48	Satin and Polished Ebony	15,899	15,558
U1SH2		48	Satin American Walnut	17,999	17,698
U1SH2		48	Polished Mahogany/White	17,999	17,698
U1TA2		48	Polished Ebony	17,899	17,558
YUS1SH2		48	Satin and Polished Ebony	20,099	18,698
YUS1SH2		48	Satin American Walnut	23,299	21,630
YUS1SH2		48	Polished Mahogany/White	23,299	21,630
YUS1TA2		48	Polished Ebony	22,099	20,698
U3SH2		52	Polished Ebony	19,059	17,798
U3SH2		52	Polished Mahogany	21,099	20,098
U3SH2		52	Satin American Walnut	21,099	20,098
YUS3SH2		52	Polished Ebony	23,399	21,698
YUS3SH2		52	Polished Mahogany	26,299	24,298
YUS3TA2		52	Polished Ebony	25,399	23,698
YUS5SH2		52	Polished Ebony	25,499	23,678
YUS5TA2		52	Polished Ebony	27,499	15,678
Grands					
GB1K	5		Polished Ebony	14,999	14,158
GB1K	5		Polished American Walnut/Mahogany/White	17,339	16,198
GB1K	5		French Provincial Satin Cherry	19,179	18,598
GB1K	5		Georgian Satin Mahogany	18,359	18,198
GC1M	5	3	Satin and Polished Ebony	23,999	23,858
GC1M	5	3	Satin American Walnut	30,599	28,198
GC1M	5	3	Polished Mahogany/White	30,599	28,198
C1X	5	3	Satin and Polished Ebony	37,999	34,098
C1X	5	3	Satin American Walnut	46,369	41,118
C1X	5	3	Polished Mahogany/White	46,369	41,118
GC2	5	8	Satin and Polished Ebony	28,959	26,998
GC2	5	8	Satin American Walnut	33,859	31,198
GC2	5	8	Polished Mahogany/White	33,859	31,198
C2X	5	8	Satin and Polished Ebony	43,999	40,198
C2X	5	8	Polished Ebony w/Chrome Accents	45,699	41,398
C2X	5	8	Satin American Walnut	53,399	47,938
C2X	5	8	Polished Mahogany/White	53,399	47,938
C3X	6	1	Satin and Polished Ebony	57,999	52,298
C3X	6	1	Satin American Walnut	69,999	62,798
C3X	6	1	Polished Mahogany/White	69,999	62,798

Model	Feet	Inches	Description	MSRP	SMP
YAMAHA *(continued)*					
S3X	6	1	Polished Ebony	77,999	74,998
CF4	6	3	Polished Ebony	105,599	105,599
C5X	6	7	Satin and Polished Ebony	63,899	58,098
C5X	6	7	Satin American Walnut	77,799	69,560
C5X	6	7	Polished Mahogany/White	77,799	69,560
S5X	6	7	Polished Ebony	84,999	80,998
C6X	7		Satin and Polished Ebony	71,199	64,698
C6X	7		Satin American Walnut	85,999	77,718
C6X	7		Polished Mahogany/White	85,999	77,718
S6X	7		Polished Ebony	95,599	92,998
CF6	7		Polished Ebony	119,999	119,598
C7X	7	6	Satin and Polished Ebony	82,999	74,698
C7X	7	6	Satin American Walnut	99,999	89,478
C7X	7	6	Polished Mahogany/White	99,999	89,478
S7X	7	6	Polished Ebony	104,999	100,998
CFX	9		Polished Ebony	179,999	179,999
Disklavier Grands					
DGB1KENCL	5		Classic Polished Ebony (playback only)	23,999	23,158
DGB1KENST	5		Polished Ebony	28,599	26,758
DGB1KENST	5		Polished Mahogany/American Walnut/White	30,939	28,798
DGC1ENST	5	3	Satin and Polished Ebony	41,699	39,558
DGC1ENST	5	3	Satin American Walnut	48,299	43,898
DGC1ENST	5	3	Polished Mahogany/White	48,299	43,898
DC1XENST	5	3	Satin and Polished Ebony	55,699	49,798
DC1XENST	5	3	Satin American Walnut	64,069	56,818
DC1XENST	5	3	Polished Mahogany/White	64,069	56,818
DGC2ENST	5	8	Satin and Polished Ebony	46,659	42,698
DGC2ENST	5	8	Satin American Walnut	51,559	46,898
DGC2ENST	5	8	Polished Mahogany/White	51,559	46,898
DC2XENST	5	8	Satin and Polished Ebony	61,699	55,898
DC2XENST	5	8	Polished Ebony w/Chrome Accents	63,399	57,098
DC2XENST	5	8	Satin American Walnut	71,099	63,638
DC2XENST	5	8	Polished Mahogany/White	71,099	63,638
DC3XENPRO	6	1	Satin and Polished Ebony	80,899	71,098
DC3XENPRO	6	1	Satin American Walnut	92,899	81,598
DC3XENPRO	6	1	Polished Mahogany/White	92,899	81,598
DS3XENPRO	6	1	Polished Ebony	117,999	112,998
DCF4ENPRO	6	3	Polished Ebony	145,599	144,198
DC5XENPRO	6	7	Satin and Polished Ebony	86,799	76,898
DC5XENPRO	6	7	Satin American Walnut	100,699	88,360
DC5XENPRO	6	7	Polished Mahogany/White	100,699	88,360
DS5XENPRO	6	7	Polished Ebony	124,999	118,998
DC6XENPRO	7		Satin and Polished Ebony	94,099	83,498
DC6XENPRO	7		Satin American Walnut	108,899	96,518

Model	Feet	Inches	Description	MSRP	SMP
YAMAHA (continued)					
DC6XENPRO	7		Polished Mahogany/White	108,899	96,518
DS6XENPRO	7		Polished Ebony	135,599	130,998
DCF6ENPRO	7		Polished Ebony	159,999	157,598
DC7XENPRO	7	6	Satin and Polished Ebony	105,899	93,498
DC7XENPRO	7	6	Satin American Walnut	122,899	108,278
DC7XENPRO	7	6	Polished Mahogany/White	122,899	108,278
DS7XENPRO	7	6	Polished Ebony	144,999	138,998
DCFXENPRO	9		Polished Ebony	219,999	218,998
Silent and TransAcoustic Grands					
GB1KSC2	5		Polished Ebony	19,499	17,858
GB1KSC2	5		Polished Mahogany/Walnut/White	21,839	19,898
GC1SH2	5	3	Satin and Polished Ebony	28,499	27,558
GC1SH2	5	3	Satin American Walnut	35,099	31,898
GC1SH2	5	3	Polished Mahogany/White	35,099	31,898
GC1TA2	5	3	Polished Ebony	32,499	31,558
C1XSH2	5	3	Satin and Polished Ebony	42,499	37,798
C1XSH2	5	3	Satin American Walnut	50,869	44,818
C1XSH2	5	3	Polished Mahogany/White	50,869	44,818
C1XTA2	5	3	Polished Ebony	46,499	41,798
GC2SH2	5	8	Satin and Polished Ebony	33,459	30,698
GC2SH2	5	8	Satin American Walnut	38,359	34,898
GC2SH2	5	8	Polished Mahogany/White	38,359	34,898
C2XSH2	5	8	Satin and Polished Ebony	48,499	43,898
C2XSH2	5	8	Polished Ebony w/Chrome Accents	50,199	45,098
C2XSH2	5	8	Satin American Walnut	57,899	51,638
C2XSH2	5	8	Polished Mahogany/White	57,899	51,638
C3XSH2	6	1	Satin and Polished Ebony	62,499	55,998
C3XSH2	6	1	Satin American Walnut	74,499	66,498
C3XSH2	6	1	Polished Mahogany/White	74,499	66,498
C3XTA2	6	1	Polished Ebony	66,499	59,998
C5XSH2	6	7	Satin and Polished Ebony	68,399	61,798
C5XSH2	6	7	Satin American Walnut	82,299	73,260
C5XSH2	6	7	Polished Mahogany/White	82,299	73,260
C6XSH2	7		Satin and Polished Ebony	75,699	68,398
C6XSH2	7		Satin American Walnut	90,499	81,418
C6XSH2	7		Polished Mahogany/White	90,499	81,418
C7XSH2	7	6	Satin and Polished Ebony	87,499	78,398
C7XSH2	7	6	Satin American Walnut	104,499	93,178
C7XSH2	7	6	Polished Mahogany/White	104,499	93,178

Model	Feet	Inches	Description	MSRP	SMP

YOUNG CHANG

Verticals

Model	Feet	Inches	Description	MSRP	SMP
Y114		45	Polished Ebony	5,990	5,900
Y114		45	Polished Mahogany	6,450	6,100
Y116		46	Polished Ebony	7,490	6,900
Y116		46	Satin Ebony/Walnut	7,590	7,000
Y121		48	Polished Ebony	7,090	6,500
Y121		48	Polished Mahogany/White	7,090	6,700
Y131		52	Polished Ebony	7,590	6,900
Y131		52	Polished Mahogany	7,790	7,100

Grands

Model	Feet	Inches	Description	MSRP	SMP
Y150	4	11	Polished Ebony	13,290	11,580
Y150	4	11	Polished Mahogany/Walnut/White	13,790	11,980
Y150SP	4	11	Polished White w/Chrome	14,090	12,780
Y157	5	2	Polished Ebony	14,390	12,780
Y157	5	2	Polished Mahogany	14,990	13,380
Y175	5	9	Polished Ebony	16,390	14,180
Y185	6	1	Polished Ebony	20,390	17,180

ZIMMERMANN

Verticals

Model	Feet	Inches	Description	MSRP	SMP
S 2		47.6	Polished Ebony	8,590	8,440
S 6		49.6	Polished Ebony	9,590	9,166

Grands

Model	Feet	Inches	Description	MSRP	SMP
Z 160	5	3	Polished Ebony	20,900	20,397
Z 175	5	9	Polished Ebony	22,900	22,848
Z 185	6	1	Polished Ebony	24,900	24,299

Digital Piano
Specifications & Prices

In the specification chart for each brand of digital piano, we have included those features and specifications about which buyers, in our experience, are most likely to be curious. However, many models have more features than are shown. See the various articles on digital pianos on our website for more information about each of the terms defined below, shown in the order in which they appear in the charts.

Form The physical form of the model: G=Grand, V= Vertical (Console), S=Slab.

Ensemble A digital piano with easy-play and auto-accompaniments (not just rhythms).

Finish The wood finishes or colors available for a particular model (not always specified for slab models). Multiple finish options are separated by a slash (/). A manufacturer's own color term is used where a generic term could not be determined. See the box below for finish codes.

FINISH CODES			
A	Ash	**O**	Oak
AG	Amber Glow	**Or**	Orange
Al	Alder	**P**	Polished (used with a wood or color designation)
Bl	Blue		
Bk	Black	**Pk**	Pink
C	Cherry	**R**	Rosewood
DB	Deep Brunette	**Rd**	Red
E	Ebony	**S**	Satin (used with a wood or color designation)
G	Gold		
Iv	Ivory	**Sr**	Silver
L	Lacquer (used with a wood or color designation)	**VR**	Velvette Rouge
		W	Walnut
M	Mahogany	**WG**	Wood Grain (wood type not specified)
MD	Mahogany Decor	**Wt**	White

Estimated Price This is our estimate of the price you will pay for the instrument. For digitals sold online or through chain and warehouse outlets, this price is the Minimum Advertised Price (MAP) and is shown in italics. For digitals sold only through bricks-and-mortar piano dealers, the price shown is based on a profit margin that piano dealers typically aspire to when selling digitals, including an allowance for incoming freight and setup. Discounts from this price, if any, typically are small. For more information on MAP and other pricing issues, please read "Buying a Digital Piano," on *www.pianobuyer.com*.

MSRP Manufacturer's Suggested Retail Price, also known as "list" or "sticker" price. Not all manufacturers use them.

Sound Source Indicates whether the sound source is Sampling (S) or Physical Modeling (M).

Voices The number of different musical voices the user can select from the instrument panel, plus (if applicable) the number of General MIDI (GM) or XG voices that are not user-selectable but are available for playback of MIDI files.

Key Release Indicates the presence of samples or simulation of Key Off sounds—acoustic piano keys and dampers returning to rest position and cutting off the sounds of vibrating strings.

Sustain Resonance Indicates the presence of samples or simulation of the sound with the sustain pedal depressed (allowing the strings to vibrate sympathetically).

String Resonance Indicates the presence of samples or simulation of String Resonance—the resonance sound of the strings of non-played notes.

Rhythms/Styles The number of rhythms in a standard digital, or the number of auto-accompaniment styles available in an ensemble digital.

Polyphony The maximum number of sounds the instrument can produce simultaneously. UL=Unlimited

Total Watts Total combined amplifier power.

Speakers The number of individual speakers.

Piano Pedals The number of piano pedals supplied with the model. A number in parentheses indicates the availability of an optional pedal unit with additional pedals.

Half Pedal Indicates that the model supports half-pedaling.

Action Indicates the type of action used, if specified.

Triple-Sensor Keys Indicates the presence of three key sensors, instead of the usual two, for greater touch realism.

Escapement Indicates the presence of an acoustic piano action's escapement feel.

Wood Keys Indicates actions with wooden keys.

Ivory Texture Indicates actions with ivory-textured keytops.

Bluetooth Indicates that the instrument is equipped with Bluetooth for connecting to theInternet.

Vocal Support The model supports some level of vocal performance. This support can vary from the piano simply having a microphone input, to its having the ability to produce the vocalist's voice in multi-part harmony, to pitch-correct the notes sung by the vocalist, or to alter the original voice.

Educational Features The model includes features that specifically support the learning experience. Note that while the ability to record and play back is an important learning tool, it is present on almost all models and so is not included in this definition.

External Storage Indicates the type of external memory storage accessible, such as USB or SanDisk.

USB to Computer Indicates the model's ability to interface with a Mac or PC via USB cable.

USB Digital Audio Indicates the ability to record and play back digital audio via a USB flash drive.

Recording Tracks The number of internal recordable tracks for recording of MIDI files.

Warranty (Parts/Labor) Indicates the manufacturer's warranty coverage period: the first number is the length of the parts coverage; the second number is the length of the labor coverage.

Dimensions Width, Depth, and Height are rounded to the nearest inch.

Weight Weight of the model rounded to the nearest pound.

Brand & Model	Form	Ensemble	Finish	Estimated Price	MSRP	Sound Source	Voices	Key Release	Sustain Resonance	String Resonance	Rhythms/Styles	Polyphony	Total Watts	Speakers	Piano Pedals	Half Pedal
Artesia																
Performer	S		Bk	200		S	12	Y	Y			32	15	4	1	Y
PA-88H	S		Bk/Wt	379		S	16	Y	Y			64	20	2	1	Y
PE-88	S		Bk	299		S	137	Y	Y		100	64	15	4	1 (2)	Y
Harmony	V		Bk	495		S	16	Y	Y			64	20	2	3	Y
DP-2	V		R	599		S	8	Y	Y			64	25	4	2	Y
DP-3	V		R	699		S	8	Y	Y			64	25	2	3	Y
DP-150e	V	E	EP/R	850		S	137	Y	Y		100	64	40	4	3	Y
AG-30	G	E	EP	1,499		S	137	Y	Y		100	128	60	6	3	Y
AG-50	G	E	EP	2,399		S	137	Y	Y		100	128	75	6	3	Y
Blüthner																
e3	V		ES/WtS	6,508	7,358	S	25+ 127GM	Y	Y	Y		256	150	4	3	Y
e3	V		EP	7,502	8,637	S	25+ 127GM	Y	Y	Y		256	150	4	3	Y
Pianette	V		EP	17,816	21,117	S	35+ 256GM	Y	Y	Y		256	150	4	3	Y
Homeline	V		ES	4,322	4,701	S	35+ 256GM	Y	Y	Y		256	60	4	3	Y
Homeline	V		MS	4,599	5,037	S	35+ 256GM	Y	Y	Y		256	60	4	3	Y
Homeline	V		BeechS	4,875	5,373	S	35+ 256GM	Y	Y	Y		256	60	4	3	Y
Sonus	V		Bk/Wt	5,650	6,397	S	40+ 256GM	Y	Y	Y		256	100	4	3	Y
Sonus	V		Bk & EP front	6,179	7,037	S	40+ 256GM	Y	Y	Y		256	100	4	3	Y
Sonus	V		EP	6,708	7,677	S	40+ 256GM	Y	Y	Y		256	100	4	3	Y
e-Grand Studio	G		ES/WtS	13,857	15,997	S	35+ 256GM	Y	Y	Y		256	150	4	3	Y
e-Grand Studio	G		EP/WtP	13,767	15,960	S	35+ 256GM	Y	Y	Y		256	150	4	3	Y
e-Grand Concert	G		ES/WtS	16,478	19,168	S	35+ 256GM	Y	Y	Y		256	150	6	3	Y
e-Grand Concert	G		EP/WtP	19,261	22,638	S	35+ 256GM	Y	Y	Y		256	150	6	3	Y
e-Grand Concert	G		EP/WtP	19,261	22,638	S	35+ 256GM	Y	Y	Y		256	150	6	3	Y
Casio																
PX-5S	S		Wt	999	1,399	S	242+ 128GM	Y	Y	Y		256	0	0	1 (2)	
PX-360	S	E	Bk	899	1,199	S	422+ 128GM	Y	Y	Y	200	128	16	4	1 (3)	Y

Brand & Model	Action	Triple-Sensor Keys	Escapement	Wood Keys	Ivory Texture	Bluetooth	Vocal Support	Educational Features	External Storage	USB to Computer	USB Digital Audio	Recording Tracks	Warranty (Parts/Labor)	Dimensions WxDxH (Inches)	Weight (Pounds)
Artesia															
Performer	Soft Touch Spring Tension	Y			Y				USB	Y	Y	0	1/3	50x11x3	22
PA-88H	Weighted Hammer Action	Y			Y				USB	Y	Y	0	1/3	52x14x5	29
PE-88	Semi-Weighted Spring Action	Y			Y			Y	USB	Y	Y	2	1/3	55x13x7	27
Harmony	Weighted Hammer Action	Y			Y				USB	Y	Y	0	1/3	58x20x9	48
DP-2	Graded Hammer Action	Y			Y			Y	USB	Y	Y	2	3/3	54x40x17	132
DP-3	Graded Hammer Action	Y			Y			Y	USB	Y	Y	2	3/3	59x22x14	132
DP-150e	Graded Hammer Action	Y		Y	Y			Y	USB	Y	Y	2	3/3	59x25x15	154
AG-30	Graded Hammer Action	Y		Y	Y			Y	USB	Y	Y	2	3/3	56x33x36	170
AG-50	Graded Hammer Action	Y		Y	Y			Y	USB	Y	Y	2	3/3	56x48x36	240
Blüthner															
PRO-88 EX	4-zone graded				Y		Y		USB	Y	Y	1	2	55x17x5	30
e3	4-zone graded			Y	Y	Y			USB	Y	Y	1	2	55x25x42	230
e3	4-zone graded			Y	Y	Y			USB	Y	Y	1	2	55x25x42	230
Pianette	4-zone graded			Y	Y	Y			USB	Y	Y	1	2	55x25x42	220
Homeline	4-zone graded	Y			Y				USB	Y	Y	1	2	55x25x42	220
Homeline	4-zone graded	Y			Y				USB	Y	Y	1	2	55x25x42	220
Homeline	4-zone graded	Y			Y				USB	Y	Y	1	2	55x25x42	220
Sonus	4-zone graded	Y	Y		Y				USB	Y	Y	1	2	56x16x41	220
Sonus	4-zone graded	Y	Y		Y				USB	Y	Y	1	2	56x16x41	220
Sonus	4-zone graded	Y	Y		Y				USB	Y	Y	1	2	56x16x41	220
e-Grand Studio	4-zone graded			Y	Y	Y			USB	Y	Y	1	2	51x33x35	225
e-Grand Studio	4-zone graded			Y	Y	Y			USB	Y	Y	1	2	51x33x35	225
e-Grand Concert	4-zone graded			Y	Y	Y			USB	Y	Y	1	2	51x55x35	248
e-Grand Concert	4-zone graded			Y	Y	Y			USB	Y	Y	1	2	51x55x35	248
Casio															
PX-5S	Weighted, Scaled, Hammer Action	Y			Y				USB	Y	Y	8	3/3	52x11x5	24
PX-360	Weighted, Scaled, Hammer Action	Y			Y			Y	USB	Y	Y	17	3/3	52x12x6	26

Casio (continued)

Brand & Model	Form	Ensemble	Finish	Estimated Price	MSRP	Sound Source	Voices	Key Release	Sustain Resonance	String Resonance	Rhythms/Styles	Polyphony	Total Watts	Speakers	Piano Pedals	Half Pedal
PX-560	S	E	Bl	1,199	1,599	S	522+128GM	Y	Y	Y	230	256	16	4	1 (3)	Y
PX-770	V		Bk/W/Wt	749	1,149	S	19		Y			128	16	2	3	Y
PX-780	V	E	Bk	899	1,399	S	122+128GM		Y	Y	180	128	40	4	3	Y
PX-870	V		Bk/W/Wt	999	1,499	S	19	Y	Y	Y		256	40	4	3	Y
PX-S1000	S		Bk/Wt/Rd	649	949	S	18	Y	Y	Y		192	16	2	1 (3)	Y
PX-S3000	S	E	Bk	849	1,149	S	572+128GM	Y	Y	Y	200	192	16	2	1 (3)	Y
CDP-S150	S	E	Bk	479	779	S	10		Y			64	16	2	1 (3)	Y
CDP-S350	S	E	Bk	549	849	S	572+128GM		Y		200	64	16	2	1 (3)	Y
AP-270	V		Bk/W/Wt	1,049	1,499	S	22		Y			192	16	2	3	Y
AP-470	V		Bk/W/Wt	1,499	1,899	S	22	Y	Y	Y		256	40	4	3	Y
AP-650	V	E	Bk	1,899	2,299	S	122+128GM	Y	Y	Y	180	256	60	4	3	Y
AP-710	V		Bk	2,499	2,999	S	26	Y	Y	Y		256	60	6	3	Y
GP-310	V		Bk/Wt	3,636	3,999	S	26	Y	Y	Y		256	100	6	3	Y
GP-510	V		BkP	4,909	5,999	S	35	Y	Y	Y		256	100	6	3	Y

Dexibell

Brand & Model	Form	Ensemble	Finish	Estimated Price	MSRP	Sound Source	Voices	Key Release	Sustain Resonance	String Resonance	Rhythms/Styles	Polyphony	Total Watts	Speakers	Piano Pedals	Half Pedal
VIVO P7	S	E	Bk	1,799	1,999	M/S	79	Y	Y	Y		UL	70	2	0 (2)	Y
VIVO S7 PRO	S	E	Wt	2,499	2,799	M/S	113	Y	Y	Y		UL		0	1 (3)	Y
VIVO S7 PRO M	S	E	Wt	2,999	3,499	M/S	113	Y	Y	Y		UL	70	2	1 (3)	Y
VIVO S9	S	E	Wt	3,999	4,499	M/S	185	Y	Y	Y		UL		0	1 (3)	Y
VIVO H1	S	E	Bk	2,634	2,799	M/S	79	Y	Y	Y		UL	70	2	3	Y
VIVO H3	V	E	Bk/Wt	2,899	2,899	M/S	79	Y	Y	Y		UL	70	4	3	Y
VIVO H7	V	E	Bk/Wt	3,999	3,999	M/S	79	Y	Y	Y		UL	112	5	3	Y
VIVO H7	V	E	Rd	4,199	4,199	M/S	79	Y	Y	Y		UL	112	5	3	Y
VIVO H7	V	E	EP/WtP/RdP	4,499	4,499	M/S	79	Y	Y	Y		UL	112	5	3	Y
VIVO H10	V	E	Bk/EP/RdP			M/S	125	Y	Y	Y		UL	112	5	3	Y

Brand & Model	Action	Triple-Sensor Keys	Escapement	Wood Keys	Ivory Texture	Bluetooth	Vocal Support	Educational Features	External Storage	USB to Computer	USB Digital Audio	Recording Tracks	Warranty (Parts/Labor)	Dimensions WxDxH (Inches)	Weight (Pounds)

Casio *(continued)*

Brand & Model	Action	Triple-Sensor Keys	Escapement	Wood Keys	Ivory Texture	Bluetooth	Vocal Support	Educational Features	External Storage	USB to Computer	USB Digital Audio	Recording Tracks	Warranty (Parts/Labor)	Dimensions WxDxH (Inches)	Weight (Pounds)
PX-560	Weighted, Scaled, Hammer Action	Y			Y			Y	USB	Y	Y	17	3/3	52x12x6	27
PX-770	Weighted, Scaled, Hammer Action	Y			Y			Y			Y	12	3/3	55x12x31	69
PX-780	Weighted, Scaled, Hammer Action	Y			Y			Y	USB	Y	Y	17	3/3	53x12x33	70
PX-870	Weighted, Scaled, Hammer Action	Y			Y			Y	USB	Y	Y	2	3/3	55x12x30	76
PX-S1000	Weighted, Scaled, Hammer Action				Y	Y		Y	USB	Y		2	3/3	52x9x4	25
PX-S3000	Weighted, Scaled, Hammer Action				Y	Y		Y	USB	Y	Y	3	3/3	52x9x4	25
CDP-S150	Weighted, Scaled, Hammer Action	Y			Y			Y	USB	Y	Y	1	1/1	52x9x4	23
CDP-S350	Weighted, Scaled, Hammer Action				Y			Y	USB	Y		6	3/3	52x9x4	24
AP-270	Weighted, Scaled, Hammer Action	Y			Y			Y			Y	2	5/5	56x17x32	81
AP-470	Weighted, Scaled, Hammer Action	Y			Y			Y	USB	Y	Y	2	5/5	54x17x33	96
AP-650	Weighted, Scaled, Hammer Action	Y			Y			Y	USB	Y	Y	17	5/5	54x17x36	111
AP-710	Weighted, Scaled, Hammer Action	Y			Y			Y	USB	Y	Y	2	5/5	54x17x36	106
GP-310	Weighted, Scaled, Hammer Action	Y	Y	Y				Y	USB	Y	Y	2	5/5	57x19x38	171
GP-510	Weighted, Scaled, Hammer Action	Y		Y	Y			Y	USB	Y	Y	2	5/5	57x19x38	171

Dexibell

Brand & Model	Action	Triple-Sensor Keys	Escapement	Wood Keys	Ivory Texture	Bluetooth	Vocal Support	Educational Features	External Storage	USB to Computer	USB Digital Audio	Recording Tracks	Warranty (Parts/Labor)	Dimensions WxDxH (Inches)	Weight (Pounds)
VIVO P7	Weighted	Y			Y			Y	USB	Y	Y	0	3	52x15x5	32
VIVO S7 PRO	Progressive Hammer	Y		Y	Y			Y	USB	Y	Y	0	3	50x14x5	39
VIVO S7 PRO M	Progressive Hammer	Y			Y			Y	USB	Y	Y	0	3	50x15x5	34
VIVO S9	Progressive Hammer	Y		Y	Y	Y		Y	USB	Y	Y	0	3	59x21x9	49
VIVO H1	Weighted	Y						Y	USB	Y	Y	0	5	56x14x31	99
VIVO H3	Weighted	Y			Y			Y	USB	Y	Y	0	5	56x14x31	97
VIVO H7	Weighted, graded	Y		Y	Y			Y	USB	Y	Y	0	5	56x14x31	137
VIVO H7	Weighted, graded	Y		Y	Y			Y	USB	Y	Y	0	5	56x14x31	137
VIVO H7	Weighted, graded	Y		Y	Y			Y	USB	Y	Y	0	5	56x14x31	137
VIVO H10	Weighted, graded	Y	Y		Y	Y	Y	Y	USB	Y	Y	0	5	56x15x31	121

Dynatone

Brand & Model	Form	Ensemble	Finish	Estimated Price	MSRP	Sound Source	Voices	Key Release	Sustain Resonance	String Resonance	Rhythms/Styles	Polyphony	Total Watts	Speakers	Piano Pedals	Half Pedal
SDP-600	V		EP	3,809	5,795	S	33+ 128GM		Y	Y		256	100	4	3	Y
SDP-600	V		WtP	3,991	6,095	S	33+ 128GM		Y	Y		256	100	4	3	Y
SLP-210	V		R	1,627	2,195	S	18+ 128GM					81	24	2	3	
SLP-250H	V		Bk	2,173	3,095	S	33+ 128GM		Y	Y		256	30	4	3	Y
DPR-3200H	V	E	Bk	2,900	4,195	S	138	Y	Y	Y	80	256	100	4	3	Y
DPR-3500	V	E	Bk	3,445	5,095	S	138	Y	Y	Y	80	256	100	4	3	Y
SGP-600	G		EP	5,173	7,695	S	33+ 128GM		Y	Y		256	100	4	3	Y
SGP-600	G		WtP	5,355	7,995	S	33+ 128GM		Y	Y		256	100	4	3	Y
GPR-3500	G	E	EP	5,900	8,895	S	138	Y	Y	Y	80	256	100	6	3	Y
GPR-3500	G	E	WtP	6,082	9,195	S	138	Y	Y	Y	80	256	100	6	3	Y
VGP-4000Q	G	E	EP	9,173	14,495	S	138	Y	Y	Y	80	256	100	6	3	Y
VGP-4000Q	G	E	WtP	9,355	14,795	S	138	Y	Y	Y	80	256	100	6	3	Y

Galileo

Brand & Model	Form	Ensemble	Finish	Estimated Price	MSRP	Sound Source	Voices	Key Release	Sustain Resonance	String Resonance	Rhythms/Styles	Polyphony	Total Watts	Speakers	Piano Pedals	Half Pedal
YP200	V		R	2,495	3,495	S	19		Y	Y		128	80	4	3	
YP300	V		R	2,995	3,995	S	20		Y	Y		128	100	4	3	
YP300	V		EP	3,495	4,495	S	20		Y	Y		128	100	4	3	
Milano 3	V	E	R	4,995	5,995	S	138				100	64	40	4	3	
GYP300	G		EP/MP/WtP	6,995	8,995	S	20		Y	Y		128	120	4	3	
Milano 3G	G	E	EP	5,995	7,995	S	138				100	64	120	4	3	

Kawai

Brand & Model	Form	Ensemble	Finish	Estimated Price	MSRP	Sound Source	Voices	Key Release	Sustain Resonance	String Resonance	Rhythms/Styles	Polyphony	Total Watts	Speakers	Piano Pedals	Half Pedal
ES110	S		Bk/Wt	699	999	S	19	Y	Y	Y	100	192	14	2	1 (3)	Y
ES520	S		Bk/Wt	1,199	1,699	S	34	Y	Y	Y	100	192	40	2	1 (3)	Y
ES920	S		Bk/Wt	1,599	2,499	S	38	Y	Y	Y	100	256	40	2	1 (3)	Y
MP7SE	S		Bk	1,799	2,199	S	256	Y	Y	Y	100	256	0	0	1 (3)	Y
MP11SE	S		Bk	2,799	3,299	S	40	Y	Y	Y	100	256	0	0		3	Y
VPC1	S		Bk	1,849	2,149		0						0	0	3	Y
KDP75	V		Bk/Wt	899	1,099	S	15	Y		Y		192	16	2	3	Y
KDP120	V		R/WtS/ES	1,199	1,549	S	15	Y		Y		192	40	2	3	Y

Brand & Model	Action	Triple-Sensor Keys	Escapement	Wood Keys	Ivory Texture	Bluetooth	Vocal Support	Educational Features	External Storage	USB to Computer	USB Digital Audio	Recording Tracks	Warranty (Parts/Labor)	Dimensions WxDxH (Inches)	Weight (Pounds)
Dynatone															
SDP-600	New RHA-3W	Y	Y							Y	Y	1	3/3	55x16x39	218
SDP-600	New RHA-3W	Y	Y							Y	Y	1	3/3	55x16x39	218
SLP-210	New RHA						Y			Y	Y	2	3/3	54x16x33	75
SLP-250H	ARHA-I				Y		Y			Y	Y	1	3/3	54x16x33	95
DPR-3200H	ARHA-3I	Y	Y					Y	USB	Y	Y	2	3/3	55x19x35	127
DPR-3500	New RHA-3W	Y	Y			Y	Y		USB	Y	Y	2	3/3	55x19x35	119
SGP-600	New RHA-3W	Y	Y							Y	Y	1	3/3	55x36x31	176
SGP-600	New RHA-3W	Y	Y							Y	Y	1	3/3	55x36x31	176
GPR-3500	New RHA-3W	Y	Y			Y	Y		USB	Y	Y	2	3/3	56x46x36	209
GPR-3500	New RHA-3W	Y	Y			Y	Y		USB	Y	Y	2	3/3	56x46x36	209
VGP-4000Q	New RHA-3W	Y	Y			Y	Y		USB	Y	Y	2	3/3	60x56x40	440
VGP-4000Q	New RHA-3W	Y	Y			Y	Y		USB	Y	Y	2	3/3	60x56x40	440
Galileo															
YP200	Grand Response									Y		0	4/1	54x17x39	119
YP300	Graded Hammer									Y		3	4/1	54x20x41	137
YP300	Graded Hammer									Y		3	4/1	54x20x41	137
Milano 3	Graded Hammer									Y		3	4/1	56x20x34	154
GYP300	Graded Hammer									Y		3	4/1	56x29x35	209
Milano 3G	Graded Hammer									Y		3	4/1	56x29x35	200
Kawai															
ES110	RHC				Y		Y					1	3/3	52x11x6	26
ES520	RHCII	Y			Y				USB	Y	Y	2	3/3	53x15x6	32
ES920	RHIII	Y	Y		Y	Y			USB	Y	Y	2	3/3	53x15x6	37
MP7SE	RHIII	Y	Y		Y				USB	Y	Y	1	3/1	53x13x7	45
MP11SE	GF	Y	Y	Y	Y				USB	Y	Y	1	3/1	58x18x8	72
VPC1	RM3II	Y	Y	Y	Y					Y		0	3/1	54x18x8	65
KDP75	RHC						Y			Y		1	3/3	54x16x34	77
KDP120	RHCII	Y			Y		Y			Y		1	3/3	54x16x34	86

Brand & Model	Form	Ensemble	Finish	Estimated Price	MSRP	Sound Source	Voices	Key Release	Sustain Resonance	String Resonance	Rhythms/Styles	Polyphony	Total Watts	Speakers	Piano Pedals	Half Pedal
Kawai *(continued)*																
CN29	V		R/WtS/ES	1,959	2,399	S	19	Y	Y	Y	100	192	40	2	3	Y
CN39	V		R/WtS/ES	2,699	3,399	S	355	Y	Y	Y	100	256	40	4	3	Y
CA49	V		R/WtS/ES	2,299	2,799	S	19	Y	Y	Y	100	192	40	4	3	Y
CA59	V		R/WtS/ES	3,099	3,999	S	44	Y	Y	Y	100	256	100	4	3	Y
CA79	V		R/WtS/ES	4,199	5,199	M/S	66	Y	Y	Y	100	256	100	6	3	Y
CA79	V		EP	4,799	5,899	M/S	66	Y	Y	Y	100	256	100	6	3	Y
CA99	V		R/WtS/ES	5,599	6,899	M/S	90	Y	Y	Y	100	256	135	6	3	Y
CA99	V		EP	6,399	7,899	M/S	90	Y	Y	Y	100	256	135	6	3	Y
NV5s	V		EP	8,173	9,999	M/S	90	Y	Y	Y	100	256	135	6	3	Y
NV10s	G		EP	12,445	15,999	M/S	90	Y	Y	Y	100	256	135	7	3	Y
DG30	G		EP	5,495	7,595	S	355	Y	Y	Y	100	256	40	4	3	Y
Korg																
B2	S		Bk/Wt	500	720	S	12		Y	Y		120	30	2	1 (3)	Y
B2N	S		Bk	430	620	S	12		Y	Y		120	30	2	1 (3)	Y
SP280	S		Bk/Wt	800	1,230	S	30					120	44	2	1	Y
SV-2-88	S		Bk	2,000	2,900	S	72		Y	Y		128	0	0	1	Y
SV-2-88SP	S		Wt	2,200	3,200	S	72		Y	Y		128	30	2	1	Y
D1	S		Bk	670	930	S	30	Y	Y	Y		120	0	0	1	Y
XE20	V	E	Bk	800	1,200	S	705		Y		280	184	36	2	1 (3)	Y
XE20SP	V	E	Bk	900	1,350	S	705		Y		280	184	36	2	3	Y
B2SP	V		Bk/Wt	600	870	S	12		Y	Y		120	30	2	3	Y
LP180	V		Bk/Wt	650	930	S	10					120	22	2	3	Y
LP380	V		Bk/Wt	1,150	1,160	S	30					120	44	2	3	Y
GB1 Air	V		Bk/Wt/R	1,800	1,950	S	32	Y	Y	Y		120	80	4	3	Y
C1 Air	V		Bk/Wt/R	1,450	1,600	S	30	Y	Y	Y		120	50	2	3	Y
Kurzweil																
MPS-110	S		Bk	1,070	1,399	S	152		Y		10	256	24	4	2	Y
MPS-120	S		Bk	1,290	1,799	S	152		Y		10	256	24	4	2	Y

Kawai (continued)

Brand & Model	Action	Triple-Sensor Keys	Escapement	Wood Keys	Ivory Texture	Bluetooth	Vocal Support	Educational Features	External Storage	USB to Computer	USB Digital Audio	Recording Tracks	Warranty (Parts/Labor)	Dimensions WxDxH (Inches)	Weight (Pounds)
CN29	RHIII	Y	Y		Y	Y		Y		Y		1	5/5	54x16x34	95
CN39	RHIII	Y	Y		Y	Y		Y	USB	Y	Y	2	5/5	57x18x34	119
CA49	GFC	Y	Y	Y	Y	Y		Y		Y		1	5/5	53x18x36	128
CA59	GFC	Y	Y	Y	Y	Y		Y	USB	Y	Y	2	5/5	57x18x36	145
CA79	GFIII	Y	Y	Y	Y	Y		Y	USB	Y	Y	2	5/5	57x18x37	167
CA79	GFIII	Y	Y	Y	Y	Y		Y	USB	Y	Y	2	5/5	57x18x37	174
CA99	GFIII	Y	Y	Y	Y	Y		Y	USB	Y	Y	2	5/5	57x18x39	183
CA99	GFIII	Y	Y	Y	Y	Y		Y	USB	Y	Y	2	5/5	57x18x39	196
NV5	Millennium III UP	Y	Y	Y	Y	Y		Y	USB	Y	Y	2	5/5	59x18x43	249
NV10	Millennium III GP	Y	Y	Y	Y	Y		Y	USB	Y	Y	2	5/5	58x25x36	291
DG30	RHIII	Y	Y		Y	Y		Y	USB	Y	Y	2	5/5	58x34x35	176

Korg

Brand & Model	Action	Triple-Sensor Keys	Escapement	Wood Keys	Ivory Texture	Bluetooth	Vocal Support	Educational Features	External Storage	USB to Computer	USB Digital Audio	Recording Tracks	Warranty (Parts/Labor)	Dimensions WxDxH (Inches)	Weight (Pounds)
B2	NH						Y			Y		0	1/1	52x14x5	26
B2N	NH						Y			Y		0	1/1	52x14x5	21
SP280	NH											0	1/1	54x16x31	42
SV-2-88	RH3									Y		0	1/1	53x14x6	45
SV-2-88SP	RH3									Y		0	1/1	53x14x6	48
D1	RH3											0	1/1	53x11x5	36
XE20	NH									Y		12	1/1	52x14x30	26
XE20SP	NH									Y		12	1/1	52x14x30	47
B2SP	NH						Y			Y		0	1/1	52x14x30	47
LP180	NH											0	1/1	54x11x31	51
LP380	RH3						Y					0	5/5	53x14x30	82
GB1 Air	RH3					Y	Y			Y		2	5/5	53x15x33	91
C1 Air	RH3					Y	Y			Y		2	5/5	53x14x31	78

Kurzweil

Brand & Model	Action	Triple-Sensor Keys	Escapement	Wood Keys	Ivory Texture	Bluetooth	Vocal Support	Educational Features	External Storage	USB to Computer	USB Digital Audio	Recording Tracks	Warranty (Parts/Labor)	Dimensions WxDxH (Inches)	Weight (Pounds)
MPS-110	Weighted, graded	Y			Y					Y	Y	0	3/2	52x15x5	36
MPS-120	Weighted, graded	Y		Y	Y					Y	Y	0	3/2	52x15x5	38

Kurzweil (continued)

Brand & Model	Form	Ensemble	Finish	Estimated Price	MSRP	Sound Source	Voices	Key Release	Sustain Resonance	String Resonance	Rhythms/Styles	Polyphony	Total Watts	Speakers	Piano Pedals	Half Pedal
KA-90	S	E	Bk	700	859	S	20	Y			50	128	60	4	1	
CUP-1	V		EP	3,200	4,399	S	1	Y	Y	Y		256	100	4	3	Y
CUP-410	V		R/Wt	2,000	2,799	S	50	Y	Y	Y		256	70	4	3	Y
KAG-100	G	E	EP	2,700	4,399	S	200	Y			100	64	35	4	3	
MPG-100	G	E	EP	4,300	6,499	S	500	Y			200	128	60	4	3	Y

Nord

Brand & Model	Form	Ensemble	Finish	Estimated Price	MSRP	Sound Source	Voices	Key Release	Sustain Resonance	String Resonance	Rhythms/Styles	Polyphony	Total Watts	Speakers	Piano Pedals	Half Pedal
Nord Piano 4	S		Rd	2,999	3,399	S	400	Y	Y			120	0	0	3	Y
Nord Grand	S		Rd/Bk	3,699	4,499	S	400	Y	Y			120	0	0	3	Y

Pearl River

Brand & Model	Form	Ensemble	Finish	Estimated Price	MSRP	Sound Source	Voices	Key Release	Sustain Resonance	String Resonance	Rhythms/Styles	Polyphony	Total Watts	Speakers	Piano Pedals	Half Pedal
GP1100	G	E	PE/PWt/PRd	4,264	5,995	S	26	Y	Y	Y	30	512	85	4	3	Y

Physis

Brand & Model	Form	Ensemble	Finish	Estimated Price	MSRP	Sound Source	Voices	Key Release	Sustain Resonance	String Resonance	Rhythms/Styles	Polyphony	Total Watts	Speakers	Piano Pedals	Half Pedal
H1	S		Alu	2,995	4,995	M	192	Y	Y	Y		UL	0	0	3	Y
H2	S		Alu	2,295	4,295	M	192	Y	Y	Y		UL	0	0	3	Y
K4EX	S		Bl	2,640	3,795	M	192	Y	Y	Y		UL	0	0	3	Y
V100	V		PE/PRd/PWt/SG/PBl	6,899	9,695	M	192	Y	Y	Y		UL	150	6	3	Y
G1000	G		EP			M	192	Y	Y	Y		UL	160	6	3	Y

Roland

Brand & Model	Form	Ensemble	Finish	Estimated Price	MSRP	Sound Source	Voices	Key Release	Sustain Resonance	String Resonance	Rhythms/Styles	Polyphony	Total Watts	Speakers	Piano Pedals	Half Pedal
RD-88	S		Bk	1,299	1,689	M/S	3000+	Y	Y	Y		128/256	12	2	1 (3)	Y
RD-2000	S		Bk	2,679	3,099	M	1100+	Y	Y	Y	200	UL/128	0	0	1 (3)	Y
V-Piano	S		Bk	6,999	7,999	M	24	Y	Y	Y		264	0	0	3	Y
GO:PIANO88	S		Bk	349	399	S	4	Y				128	20	2	1	
FP-10	S		Bk	499	649	M/S	15	Y	Y	Y		96	12	2	1	Y
FP-10C	V		Bk	589	779	M/S	15	Y	Y	Y		96	12	2	1	Y
FP-30	S	E	Bk/Wt	699	899	M/S	35	Y	Y	Y	8	128	22	2	1 (3)	Y
FP-30C	V	E	Bk/Wt	899	1,119	M/S	35	Y	Y	Y	8	128	22	2	1	Y
FP-30X	S	E	Bk/Wt	749	979	M/S	56	Y	Y	Y	21	256	22	2	1 (3)	Y
FP-60	S	E	Bk/Wt	1,499	1,799	M/S	355	Y	Y	Y	21	288	26	2	1 (3)	Y

Brand & Model	Action	Triple-Sensor Keys	Escapement	Wood Keys	Ivory Texture	Bluetooth	Vocal Support	Educational Features	External Storage	USB to Computer	USB Digital Audio	Recording Tracks	Warranty (Parts/Labor)	Dimensions WxDxH (Inches)	Weight (Pounds)
Kurzweil *(continued)*															
KA-90	Weighted									Y		1	3/2	54x14x5	27
CUP-1	Weighted, graded			Y	Y	Y				Y	Y	0	3/2	56x17x42	221
CUP-410	Weighted, graded	Y		Y		Y				Y	Y	1	3/2	55x18x36	113
KAG-100	Weighted			Y				Y	USB	Y	Y	2	3/2	56x30x35	150
MPG-100	Weighted, graded	Y						Y		Y		6	3/2	56x36x35	212
Nord															
Nord Piano 4	Fatar Weighted	Y								Y		0	1/1	51x13x5	40
Nord Grand	Kawai Weighted	Y		Y						Y		0	1/1	51x15x7	46
Pearl River															
GP1100	Fatar Weighted, Graded			Y		Y				Y		2	4/1	56x41x36	214
Physis															
H1	Tri-sensor, Hybrid	Y	Y	Y	Y				USB	Y	Y	16	3/1	54x13x4	58
H2	Lightweight Hammer, 3 sensors	Y	Y						USB	Y	Y	16	3/1	54x13x4	45
K4EX	Tri-sensor, Hybrid	Y	Y						USB	Y	Y	16	3/1	51x14x5	40
V100	Tri-sensor, Hybrid	Y	Y	Y	Y				USB	Y	Y	16	3/1	58x17x46	233
G1000	Tri-sensor, Hybrid	Y	Y	Y	Y				USB	Y		2	3/1	57x40x56	288
Roland															
RD-88	PHA-4 Standard	Y	Y				Y		USB	Y	Y		3/2	51x11x6	30
RD-2000	PHA-50 Concert	Y	Y	Y	Y				USB	Y	Y	1	3/2	56x15x6	55
V-Piano	PHA III	Y	Y		Y				USB	Y	Y	0	3/2	56x21x7	84
GO:PIANO88	Touch Sensitive					Y		Y		Y			1/90	51x11x5	16
FP-10	PHA-4 Standard	Y	Y		Y	Y	Y			Y			3/2	51x11x6	27
FP-10C	PHA-4 Standard	Y	Y		Y	Y	Y			Y			3/2	51x13x36	44
FP-30	PHA-4 Standard	Y	Y		Y	Y	Y		USB	Y		1	5/2	51x11x6	31
FP-30C	PHA-4 Standard	Y	Y		Y	Y	Y		USB	Y		1	5/2	51x13x36	57
FP-30X	PHA-4 Standard	Y	Y		Y	Y	Y		USB	Y	Y	3	5/2	51x11x6	31
FP-60	PHA-4 Standard	Y	Y		Y	Y			USB	Y	Y	1	5/2	51x14x5	42

Brand & Model	Form	Ensemble	Finish	Estimated Price	MSRP	Sound Source	Voices	Key Release	Sustain Resonance	String Resonance	Rhythms/Styles	Polyphony	Total Watts	Speakers	Piano Pedals	Half Pedal
Roland (continued)																
FP-60C	V	E	Bk/Wt	1,849	2,299 M/S	355	Y	Y	Y	21	288	26	2	3	Y
FP-60X	S	E	Bk/Wt	1,099	1,399 M/S	358	Y	Y	Y	21	256	26	2	1 (3)	Y
FP-90	S	E	Bk/Wt	2,099	2,299 M	355	Y	Y	Y	21	UL/384	60	4	1 (3)	Y
FP-90C	V	E	Bk/Wt	2,499	2,799 M	355	Y	Y	Y	21	UL/384	60	4	3	Y
FP-90X	S	E	Bk/Wt	2,199	2,599 M	362	Y	Y	Y	21	UL/256	60	4	1 (3)	Y
DP-603	V	E	Bk	2,699	2,999 M	319	Y	Y	Y	21	UL/384	24	2	3	Y
DP-603	V	E	EP/WtP	3,099	3,499 M	319	Y	Y	Y	21	UL/384	24	2	3	Y
HP-504	V		R/ES	2,199	2,499 M/S	350	Y	Y	Y		128	24	2	3	Y
HP-601	V	E	R/ES/Wt	2,299	2,799 M/S	319	Y	Y	Y	21	288	28	2	3	Y
HP-603	V	E	R/ES/Wt	2,999	3,399 M	319	Y	Y	Y	21	UL/384	60	2	3	Y
HP-603A	V	E	R/ES/Wt	3,199	3,499 M	319	Y	Y	Y	21	UL/384	60	2	3	Y
HP-605	V	E	EP	4,349	4,999 M	319	Y	Y	Y	21	UL/384	74	6	3	Y
HP-605	V	E	R/ES/Wt	3,849	4,499 M	319	Y	Y	Y	21	UL/384	74	6	3	Y
HPi-50e	V	E	R	4,499	4,999 M/S	350	Y	Y	Y	50	128	74	4	3	Y
HP-702	V	E	O/R/ES/Wt	2,399	2,399 M	324	Y	Y	Y	21	UL/384	28	2	3	Y
HP-704	V	E	O/R/ES/Wt	3,099	3,099 M	324	Y	Y	Y	21	UL/384	60	4	3	Y
HP-704	V	E	EP	3,699	3,699 M	324	Y	Y	Y	21	UL/384	60	4	3	Y
LX-7	V	E	EP	5,999	6,899 M	319	Y	Y	Y	21	UL/384	74	6	3	Y
LX-7	V	E	W/ES	5,499	6,299 M	319	Y	Y	Y	21	UL/384	74	6	3	Y
LX-17	V	E	EP	6,499	7,599 M	319	Y	Y	Y	21	UL/384	74	8	3	Y
LX-17	V	E	WtP	6,799	7,999 M	319	Y	Y	Y	21	UL/384	74	8	3	Y
LX-705	V	E	O/R/ES	3,699	3,699 M	324	Y	Y	Y	21	UL/256	60	4	3	Y
LX-705	V	E	EP	4,299	4,299 M	324	Y	Y	Y	21	UL/256	60	4	3	Y
LX-706	V	E	R/ES	4,199	4,199 M	324	Y	Y	Y	21	UL/256	74	6	3	Y
LX-706	V	E	EP	4,799	4,799 M	324	Y	Y	Y	21	UL/256	74	6	3	Y
LX-708	V	E	ES	6,199	6,199 M	324	Y	Y	Y	21	UL/256	74	8	3	Y
LX-708	V	E	EP	6,899	6,899 M	324	Y	Y	Y	21	UL/256	74	8	3	Y
LX-708	V	E	WtP	7,099	7,099 M	324	Y	Y	Y	21	UL/256	74	8	3	Y
F-140R	V	E	Bk/Wt	1,369	1,499 M/S	316	Y	Y	Y	72	128	24	2	3	Y
F-701	V	E	Bk/Wt/O	1,399	1,699 M/S	324	Y	Y	Y	21	256	24	2	3	Y

Roland *(continued)*

Brand & Model	Action	Triple-Sensor Keys	Escapement	Wood Keys	Ivory Texture	Bluetooth	Vocal Support	Educational Features	External Storage	USB to Computer	USB Digital Audio	Recording Tracks	Warranty (Parts/Labor)	Dimensions WxDxH (Inches)	Weight (Pounds)
FP-60C	PHA-4 Standard	Y	Y		Y	Y		Y	USB	Y	Y	1	5/2	51x14x37	72
FP-60X	PHA-4 Standard	Y	Y		Y	Y	Y	Y	USB	Y	Y	3	5/2	51x14x5	42
FP-90	PHA-50 Concert	Y	Y	Y	Y	Y	Y	Y	USB	Y	Y	2	5/2	53x15x5	52
FP-90C	PHA-50 Concert	Y	Y	Y	Y	Y	Y	Y	USB	Y	Y	2	5/2	53x15x37	83
FP-90X	PHA-50 Concert	Y	Y	Y	Y	Y	Y	Y	USB	Y	Y	3	5/2	53x15x5	52
DP-603	PHA-50 Concert	Y	Y	Y	Y	Y		Y	USB	Y	Y	3	5/2	55x14x31	104
DP-603	PHA-50 Concert	Y	Y	Y	Y	Y		Y	USB	Y	Y	3	5/2	55x14x31	104
HP-504	PHA4-Premium	Y	Y		Y			Y	USB	Y	Y	3	5/2	55x17x41	114
HP-601	PHA-50 Concert	Y	Y	Y	Y			Y	USB	Y	Y	3	5/2	54x17x40	110
HP-603	PHA-50 Concert	Y	Y	Y	Y			Y	USB	Y	Y	3	10/10	54x17x42	110
HP-603A	PHA-50 Concert	Y	Y	Y	Y			Y	USB	Y	Y	3	10/10	54x17x42	110
HP-605	PHA-50 Concert	Y	Y	Y	Y			Y	USB	Y	Y	3	10/10	54x17x44	119
HP-605	PHA-50 Concert	Y	Y	Y	Y			Y	USB	Y	Y	3	10/10	54x17x44	119
HPi-50e	PHA4-Concert	Y	Y		Y			Y	USB	Y	Y	16	5/2	55x17x43	127
HP-702	PHA-4 Standard	Y	Y		Y	Y		Y	USB	Y	Y	3	5/2	54x18x42	120
HP-704	PHA-50 Concert	Y	Y	Y	Y	Y		Y	USB	Y	Y	3	10/10	54x19x44	131
HP-704	PHA-50 Concert	Y	Y	Y	Y	Y		Y	USB	Y	Y	3	10/10	54x19x44	134
LX-7	PHA-50 Concert	Y	Y	Y	Y	Y		Y	USB	Y	Y	3	10/10	55x18x41	170
LX-7	PHA-50 Concert	Y	Y	Y	Y	Y		Y	USB	Y	Y	3	10/10	55x18x41	170
LX-17	PHA-50 Concert	Y	Y	Y	Y	Y			USB	Y	Y	3	10/10	55x19x42	193
LX-17	PHA-50 Concert	Y	Y	Y	Y	Y			USB	Y	Y	3	10/10	55x19x42	193
LX-705	PHA-50 Concert	Y	Y	Y	Y	Y		Y	USB	Y	Y	3	10/10	54x18x41	164
LX-705	PHA-50 Concert	Y	Y	Y	Y	Y		Y	USB	Y	Y	3	10/10	54x18x41	167
LX-706	PHA-100 Hybrid Grand	Y	Y	Y	Y	Y		Y	USB	Y	Y	3	10/10	54x19x44	212
LX-706	PHA-100 Hybrid Grand	Y	Y	Y	Y	Y		Y	USB	Y	Y	3	10/10	54x19x44	216
LX-708	PHA-100 Hybrid Grand	Y	Y	Y	Y	Y		Y	USB	Y	Y	3	10/10	55x19x46	240
LX-708	PHA-100 Hybrid Grand	Y	Y	Y	Y	Y		Y	USB	Y	Y	3	10/10	55x19x46	243
LX-708	PHA-100 Hybrid Grand	Y	Y	Y	Y	Y		Y	USB	Y	Y	3	10/10	55x19x46	243
F-140R	PHA-4-Standard	Y	Y		Y	Y		Y	USB	Y	Y	1	5/2	54x14x36	76
F-701	PHA-4-Standard	Y	Y		Y	Y		Y	USB	Y	Y	3	5/2	54x14x36	79

Brand & Model	Form	Ensemble	Finish	Estimated Price	MSRP	Sound Source	Voices	Key Release	Sustain Resonance	String Resonance	Rhythms/Styles	Polyphony	Total Watts	Speakers	Piano Pedals	Half Pedal
Roland (*continued*)																
RP-102	V	E	Bk	*949*	1,199 M/S		318	Y	Y	Y	21	128	12	2	3	Y
RP-501R	V	E	Bk/Wt/R	*1,679*	1,999 M/S		316	Y	Y	Y	72	128	24	2	3	Y
RP-701	V	E	Bk/Wt/R/O	*1,499*	1,799 M/S		324	Y	Y	Y	21	256	24	2	3	Y
GP-7 (V-Piano Grand)	G		EP	*19,950*	22,999 M		30	Y	Y	Y		264	240	8	3	Y
GP-607 (Mini Grand)	G	E	EP	5,999	5,999 M		319	Y	Y	Y	21	UL/384	70	5	3	Y
GP-607 (Mini Grand)	G	E	WtP	6,199	6,199 M		319	Y	Y	Y	21	UL/384	70	5	3	Y
GP-609 (Grand Piano)	G	E	EP	9,999	9,999 M		319	Y	Y	Y	21	UL/384	74	7	3	Y
GP-609 (Grand Piano)	G	E	WtP	10,399	10,399 M		319	Y	Y	Y	21	UL/384	74	7	3	Y
Samick																
SG-120	G	E	EP	4,179	4,595 S		377	Y	Y	Y	353	128	60	6	3	Y
SG-120	G	E	WtP	4,320	4,750 S		377	Y	Y	Y	353	128	60	6	3	Y
SG-120	G	E	RdP	4,452	4,895 S		377	Y	Y	Y	353	128	60	6	3	Y
SG-500	G	E	EP	5,230	5,750 S		377	Y	Y	Y	352	128	80	8	3	Y
SG-500	G	E	WtP	5,384	5,920 S		377	Y	Y	Y	352	128	80	8	3	Y
SG-500	G	E	RdP	5,502	6,050 S		377	Y	Y	Y	352	128	80	8	3	Y
Suzuki																
VG-88	V		R	*1,800*	1,800 S		16+ 128GM		Y	Y		189	40	4	3	
CTP-88	V	E	M	*1,200*	1,200 S		122+ 128GM		Y	Y	100	128	60	4	3	
MDG-300	G	E	EP	*2,200*	2,200 S		122+ 128GM		Y	Y	100	128	120	6	3	
MDG-330	G	E	EP	*3,000*	3,000 S		122+ 128GM		Y	Y	100	128	120	6	3	
MDG-400	G		EP	*3,300*	3,300 S		122+ 128GM		Y	Y	100	128	120	6	3	
Williams																
Legato III	S		Bk	*199*	229 S		10		Y			64	40	2	1	
Allegro III	S		Bk	*299*	329 S		10		Y			64	60	2	1	
Rhapsody 2	V		WG/EP	*499*	900 S		12		Y			64	60	2	2	

Roland (continued)

Brand & Model	Action	Triple-Sensor Keys	Escapement	Wood Keys	Ivory Texture	Bluetooth	Vocal Support	Educational Features	External Storage	USB to Computer	USB Digital Audio	Recording Tracks	Warranty (Parts/Labor)	Dimensions WxDxH (Inches)	Weight (Pounds)
RP-102	PHA4-Standard	Y	Y		Y	Y		Y		Y		0	5/2	54x17x39	83
RP-501R	PHA-4 Standard	Y	Y		Y	Y		Y	USB	Y	Y	1	5/2	54x17x39	81
RP-701	PHA-4 Standard	Y	Y		Y	Y		Y	USB	Y	Y	3	5/2	54x18x40	101
GP-7 (V-Piano Grand)	PHA III	Y	Y		Y				USB	Y	Y	1	5/2	59x59x61	375
GP-607 (Mini Grand)	PHA-50 Concert	Y	Y	Y	Y	Y		Y	USB	Y	Y	3	10/10	55x37x35	223
GP-607 (Mini Grand)	PHA-50 Concert	Y	Y	Y	Y	Y		Y	USB	Y	Y	3	10/10	55x37x35	223
GP-609 (Grand Piano)	PHA-50 Concert	Y	Y	Y	Y	Y		Y	USB	Y	Y	3	10/10	57x59x62	326
GP-609 (Grand Piano)	PHA-50 Concert	Y	Y	Y	Y	Y		Y	USB	Y	Y	3	10/10	57x59x62	326

Samick

Brand & Model	Action	Triple-Sensor Keys	Escapement	Wood Keys	Ivory Texture	Bluetooth	Vocal Support	Educational Features	External Storage	USB to Computer	USB Digital Audio	Recording Tracks	Warranty (Parts/Labor)	Dimensions WxDxH (Inches)	Weight (Pounds)
SG-120	Graded	Y			Y	Y	Y		USB	Y	Y	5	3/3	56x35x29	170
SG-120	Graded	Y			Y	Y	Y		USB	Y	Y	5	3/3	56x35x29	170
SG-120	Graded	Y			Y	Y	Y		USB	Y	Y	5	3/3	56x35x29	170
SG-500	Graded	Y			Y	Y	Y		USB	Y	Y	5	3/3	56x49x35	290
SG-500	Graded	Y			Y	Y	Y		USB	Y	Y	5	3/3	56x49x35	290
SG-500	Graded	Y			Y	Y	Y		USB	Y	Y	5	3/3	56x49x35	290

Suzuki

Brand & Model	Action	Triple-Sensor Keys	Escapement	Wood Keys	Ivory Texture	Bluetooth	Vocal Support	Educational Features	External Storage	USB to Computer	USB Digital Audio	Recording Tracks	Warranty (Parts/Labor)	Dimensions WxDxH (Inches)	Weight (Pounds)
VG-88	Graded				Y	Y			Y			1	1/1	58x19x41	236
CTP-88	Graded						Y		SD	Y		3	1/1	54x20x40	175
MDG-300	Graded						Y		SD	Y		3	1/1	55x30x36	218
MDG-330	Graded						Y		SD	Y		3	1/1	57x39x36	330
MDG-400	Graded						Y		SD	Y		3	1/1	55x49x35	315

Williams

Brand & Model	Action	Triple-Sensor Keys	Escapement	Wood Keys	Ivory Texture	Bluetooth	Vocal Support	Educational Features	External Storage	USB to Computer	USB Digital Audio	Recording Tracks	Warranty (Parts/Labor)	Dimensions WxDxH (Inches)	Weight (Pounds)
Legato III	Semi-Weighted					Y		Y		Y		0	1/1	50x11x4	19
Allegro III	Weighted					Y		Y		Y		1	1/1	52x5x13	30
Rhapsody 2	Weighted									Y		2	1/1	54x16x31	83

Brand & Model	Form	Ensemble	Finish	Estimated Price	MSRP	Sound Source	Voices	Key Release	Sustain Resonance	String Resonance	Rhythms/Styles	Polyphony	Total Watts	Speakers	Piano Pedals	Half Pedal
Williams *(continued)*																
Overture 2	V		EP/RdM	699	1,200	S	19+128GM		Y			64	60	4	3	
Symphony Grand	G	E	EP/RdM	1,499	1,999	S	46+128GM	Y	Y	Y	120	128	60	6	3	
Symphony Grand II	G	E	EP/RdM/Wt	1,999	2,299	S	44+128GM	Y	Y	Y	180	256	100	8	3	
Yamaha																
P45	S		Bk	500	599	S	10					64	12	2	1	Y
P121	S		Bk/Wt	600	899	M/S	24		Y			192		4		
P125	S		Bk/Wt	650	999	S	24				20	192	14	4	1 (3)	Y
P515	S		Bk/Wt	1,499	1,999	S	40+480XG	Y	Y	Y	40	256	40	4	1 (3)	Y
CP300	S		Bk	2,500	3,499	S	50+480XG	Y	Y	Y		128	60	2	3	Y
CP40 Stage	S		Bk	1,400	2,399	M/S	297	Y	Y			128	0	0	1 (2)	Y
CP4 Stage	S		Bk	2,000	2,699	M/S	433	Y	Y			128	0	0	1 (2)	Y
CP1	S		Bk	5,000	5,999	M/S	17	Y	Y	Y		128	0	0	3	Y
YDP144	V		BkW/R	1,100	1,499	S	10					192	12	2	3	Y
YDPS34	V		BkW/R	1,000	1,399	S	10					192	12	2	3	Y
YDP164	V		BkW/R	1,500	1,999	S	10					192	40	4	3	Y
YDPS54	V		Bk/Wt	1,350	2,199	S	10					192	40	4	3	Y
YDP184	V		R	2,200	2,799	S	24	Y	Y	Y		256	60	2	3	Y
CSP150	V	E	Bk	3,500	3,999	S	721+480XG	Y	Y	Y	470	256	60	2	3	Y
CSP150	V	E	EP	4,000	4,599	S	721+480XG	Y	Y	Y	470	256	60	2	3	Y
CSP170	V	E	Bk	4,700	5,399	S	721+480XG	Y	Y	Y	470	256	180	4	3	Y
CSP170	V	E	EP	5,300	5,999	S	721+480XG	Y	Y	Y	470	256	180	4	3	Y
CLP725	V		Bk/R	2,000	2,299	S	10	Y	Y	Y	0	256	40	2	3	Y
CLP725	V		EP	2,400	2,699	S	10	Y	Y	Y	0	256	40	2	3	Y
CLP735	V		Bk/DW/R/wt	2,700	2,999	S	38	Y	Y	Y	20	256	60	2	3	Y
CLP735	V		EP	3,200	3,599	S	38	Y	Y	Y	20	256	60	2	3	Y
CLP745	V		Bk/DW/R/Wt	3,500	3,999	S	38	Y	Y	Y	20	256	200	4	3	Y
CLP745	V		EP	4,000	4,599	S	38	Y	Y	Y	20	256	200	4	3	Y
CLP775	V		Bk/DW/R/Wt	4,700	5,199	S	38	Y	Y	Y	20	256	184	6	3	Y

Williams *(continued)*

Brand & Model	Action	Triple-Sensor Keys	Escapement	Wood Keys	Ivory Texture	Bluetooth	Vocal Support	Educational Features	External Storage	USB to Computer	USB Digital Audio	Recording Tracks	Warranty (Parts/Labor)	Dimensions WxDxH (Inches)	Weight (Pounds)
Overture 2	Weighted						Y		USB	Y		2	1/1	55x19x34	117
Symphony Grand	Weighted			Y			Y		USB	Y	Y	4	1/1	54x35x36	163
Symphony Grand II	Weighted			Y			Y		USB	Y	Y	4	1/1	55x37x38	225

Yamaha

Brand & Model	Action	Triple-Sensor Keys	Escapement	Wood Keys	Ivory Texture	Bluetooth	Vocal Support	Educational Features	External Storage	USB to Computer	USB Digital Audio	Recording Tracks	Warranty (Parts/Labor)	Dimensions WxDxH (Inches)	Weight (Pounds)
P45	GHS									Y		0	3/3	52x12x6	26
P121	GHS									Y		0	3/3	44x12x7	22
P125	GHS									Y	Y	2	3/3	52x12x6	26
P515	NWX	Y	Y	Y	Y	Y			USB	Y	Y	16	3/3	53x14x7	48
CP300	GH									Y		16	3/3	54x18x7	72
CP40 Stage	GH								USB	Y	Y	0	3/3	52x14x6	36
CP4 Stage	NW-GH3	Y		Y	Y				USB	Y	Y	0	3/3	52x14x6	39
CP1	NW-Stage			Y	Y				USB	Y		0	3/3	55x17x7	60
YDP144	GHS									Y	Y	2	3/3	54x17x33	84
YDPS34	GHS									Y	Y	2	3/3	54x17x31	80
YDP164	GH3	Y			Y					Y	Y	2	3/3	54x17x34	93
YDPS54	GH3	Y			Y					Y	Y	2	3/3	55x12x31	80
YDP184	GH3	Y			Y				USB	Y		16	3/3	57x36x18	123
CSP150	GH3X	Y	Y		Y		Y	Y	USB-Tablet	Y	Y	16	5/5	56x18x40	127
CSP150	GH3X	Y	Y		Y		Y	Y	USB-Tablet	Y	Y	17	5/6	56x18x40	127
CSP170	NWX	Y	Y	Y	Y		Y	Y	USB-Tablet	Y	Y	18	5/7	56x18x40	147
CSP170	NWX	Y	Y	Y	Y		Y	Y	USB-Tablet	Y	Y	19	5/8	56x18x40	147
CLP725	GrandTouch-S	Y	Y		Y		Y		USB	Y	Y	2	5/5	54x17x34	100
CLP725	GrandTouch-S	Y	Y		Y		Y		USB	Y	Y	2	5/5	54x17x34	100
CLP735	GrandTouch-S	Y	Y		Y		Y		USB	Y	Y	16	5/5	58x19x37	125
CLP735	GrandTouch-S	Y	Y		Y		Y		USB	Y	Y	16	5/5	58x19x37	132
CLP745	GrandTouch-S	Y	Y		Y	Y	Y		USB	Y	Y	16	5/5	58x19x37	132
CLP745	GrandTouch-S	Y	Y		Y	Y	Y		USB	Y	Y	16	5/5	58x19x37	138
CLP775	GrandTouch	Y	Y	Y	Y	Y		Y	USB	Y	Y	2	5/5	58x19x45	157

Yamaha (continued)

Brand & Model	Form	Ensemble	Finish	Estimated Price	MSRP	Sound Source	Voices	Key Release	Sustain Resonance	String Resonance	Rhythms/Styles	Polyphony	Total Watts	Speakers	Piano Pedals	Half Pedal
CLP775	V		EP	5,300	5,999	S	38	Y	Y	Y	20	256	184	6	3	Y
CLP785	V		Bk	5,800	6,499	S	53+ 480 XG	Y	Y	Y	20	256	300	6	3	Y
CLP785	V		EP	6,600	7,499	S	53+ 480 XG	Y	Y	Y	20	256	300	6	3	Y
CLP785	V		WtP	7,591	8,474	S	53+ 480 XG	Y	Y	Y	20	256	300	6	3	Y
CVP701	V	E	Bk	3,999	5,278	S	777+ 480XG	Y	Y	Y	310	256	50	2	3	Y
CVP701	V	E	EP	4,799	6,199	S	777+ 480XG	Y	Y	Y	310	256	50	2	3	Y
CVP805	V	E	Bk	7,400	9,199	S	1315+ 480XG	Y	Y	Y	525	256	130	4	3	Y
CVP805	V	E	EP	8,000	9,999	S	1315+ 480XG	Y	Y	Y	525	256	130	4	3	Y
CVP809	V	E	Bk	11,800	14,499	S	1605+ 480XG	Y	Y	Y	675	256	260	7	3	Y
CVP809	V	E	EP	12,500	14,999	S	1605+ 480XG	Y	Y	Y	675	256	260	7	3	Y
CVP809	V	E	WtP	13,000	15,999	S	1005+ 480XG	Y	Y	Y	675	256	260	7	3	Y
NU1X	V		EP	6,362	7,699	S	15	Y	Y	Y		256	180	4	3	Y
NU1X	V		WtP	6,635	7,899	S	15	Y	Y	Y		256	180	4	3	Y
N1X	G		EP	9,453	10,999	S	15	Y	Y	Y		256	180	6	3	Y
N2	G		EP	12,362	14,999	S	5	Y	Y	Y		256	500	12	3	Y
N3X	G		EP	18,816	22,199	S	10	Y	Y	Y		256	500	12	3	Y
CLP765GP	G		EP	5,500	6,199	S	38	Y	Y	Y	20	256	184	4	3	Y
CLP765GP	G		WtP	6,300	6,999	S	38	Y	Y	Y	20	256	184	4	3	Y
CLP795GP	G		EP	7,500	8,499	S	53+ 480 XG	Y	Y	Y	20	256	300	7	3	Y
CLP795GP	G		WtP	8,500	9,999	S	53+ 480 XG	Y	Y	Y	20	256	300	7	3	Y
CVP809GP	G	E	EP	16,000	19,999	S	1605+ 480XG	Y	Y	Y	675	256	260	6	3	Y
CVP809GP	G	E	WtP	17,000	21,999	S	1605+ 480XG	Y	Y	Y	675	256	260	6	3	Y

Yamaha *(continued)*

Brand & Model	Action	Triple-Sensor Keys	Escapement	Wood Keys	Ivory Texture	Bluetooth	Vocal Support	Educational Features	External Storage	USB to Computer	USB Digital Audio	Recording Tracks	Warranty (Parts/Labor)	Dimensions WxDxH (Inches)	Weight (Pounds)
CLP775	GrandTouch	Y	Y	Y	Y	Y		Y	USB	Y	Y	2	5/5	58x19x45	163
CLP785	GrandTouch-S	Y	Y	Y	Y	Y		Y	USB	Y	Y	16	5/5	58x19x41	185
CLP785	GrandTouch-S	Y	Y	Y	Y	Y		Y	USB	Y	Y	16	5/5	58x19x41	191
CLP785	GrandTouch-S	Y	Y	Y	Y	Y		Y	USB	Y	Y	16	5/5	58x19x41	185
CVP701	GH3X		Y		Y		Y	Y	USB	Y	Y	16	5/5	53x24x36	130
CVP701	GH3X	Y	Y		Y		Y	Y	USB	Y	Y	16	5/5	53x24x36	130
CVP805	GrandTouch		Y		Y	Y	Y	Y	USB	Y		16	5/5	56x24x41	185
CVP805	GrandTouch		Y		Y	Y	Y	Y	USB	Y		16	5/5	56x24x41	185
CVP809	GrandTouch		Y		Y	Y	Y	Y	USB	Y		16	5/5	56x24x41	185
CVP809	GrandTouch		Y		Y	Y	Y	Y	USB	Y		16	5/5	56x24x41	185
CVP809	GrandTouch	Y	Y	Y	Y	Y	Y	Y	USB	Y		16	5/5	56x24x41	185
NU1X	Specialized Upright		Y		Y				USB	Y	Y	1	5/5	60x18x40	240
NU1X	Specialized Upright		Y		Y				USB	Y	Y	1	5/5	60x18x40	240
N1X	Specialized Grand	Y	Y		Y				USB	Y	Y	1	5/5	58x24x39	257
N2	Specialized Grand	Y	Y	Y					USB			1	5/5	58x21x40	313
N3X	Specialized Grand	Y	Y	Y					USB	Y	Y	1	5/5	58x47x40	439
CLP765GP	GrandTouch-S	Y	Y		Y	Y		Y	USB	Y	Y	16	5/5	57x46x48	234
CLP765GP	GrandTouch-S	Y	Y		Y	Y		Y	USB	Y	Y	16	5/5	57x46x48	234
CLP795GP	GrandTouch-S	Y	Y	Y	Y	Y		Y	USB	Y	Y	16	5/5	57x49x63	278
CLP795GP	GrandTouch-S	Y	Y	Y	Y	Y		Y	USB	Y	Y	16	5/5	57x49x63	278
CVP809GP	GrandTouch	Y	Y	Y	Y	Y	Y	Y	USB	Y	Y	16	5/5	56x48x42	275
CVP809GP	GrandTouch	Y	Y	Y	Y	Y	Y	Y	USB	Y	Y	16	5/5	56x48x42	275